Updated 2024

Egyptian Mystics

Seekers of The Way

Moustafa Gadalla

CONTENTS

PART IV : COME ONE COME ALL

1

ABOUT THE AUTHOR

Moustafa Gadalla is an Egyptian-American independent Egyp-tologist who was born in Cairo, Egypt in 1944. He holds a Bache-lor of Science degree in civil engineering from Cairo University.

From his early childhood, Gadalla pursued his Ancient Egyptian roots with passion, through continuous study and research. Since 1990, he has dedicated and concentrated all his time to researching and writing.

Gadalla is the author of twenty-two published internationally acclaimed books about the various aspects of the Ancient Egypt-ian history and civilization and its influences worldwide. In addition he operates a multimedia resource center for accurate, educative studies of Ancient Egypt, presented in an engaging, practical, and interesting manner that appeals to the general pub-lic.

He was the Founder of Tehuti Research Foundation which was later incorporated into the multi-lingual Egyptian Wisdom Center (https://www.egyptianwisdomcenter.org) in more than ten languages.The website also includes another ongoing activity; his creation and production of performing arts projects such as the Isis Rises Operetta, Horus The Initiate Operetta; Egyptian Goddesses Operetta; and a few more other productions to follow.

2

PREFACE [2ND EDITION]

This book being the Second Edition, is a revised and expanded edition of the First Edition of *Egyptian Mystics: Seekers of The Way*, published in 2003.

This book explains how Ancient Egypt is the origin of alchemy and present-day Sufism, and how the mystics of Egypt camouflage their practices with a thin layer of Islam. The book also explains the progression of the mystical Way towards enlightenment, providing a coherent explanation of its fundamentals and practices. It shows the correspondence between the Ancient Egyptian calendar of events and the cosmic cycles of the universe.

It is the aim of this book to provide such an exposition; one which, while based on sound scholarship, will present the issues in language comprehensible to non-specialist readers. Technical terms have been kept to a minimum. These are explained, as non-technically as possible, in the glossary. This Expanded Version of the book is divided into four parts containing a total of 13 chapters and three appendices.

Part I: The Hidden treasure consists of two chapters:

    Chapter 1: Egyptian Mysticism and Islamized Sufism will

cover the differences between dogmatic and mystical routes and how ancient Egypt is the source of Sufism and alchemy.

Chapter 2: The Treasure Within will cover the limitations of humans organ of perceptions and how to find realities with such limitations.

Part II: Transformation From Dust To Gold consists of five chapters—3 through 7:

Chapter 3: The Alchemist Way will cover the source of alchemy as being from Ancient Egypt; the progression along the alchemist way; and the role of a guide in the process.

Chapter 4: The Purification Process will cover both outer and inner purifications through the process of living in the world.

Chapter 5: Basic Practices will cover general practices by the Egyptian mystics to increase their awareness of the real world.

Chapter 6: The Way to Revelations will cover the methods by which a mystical aspirant can find knowledge through revelations.

Chapter 7: The Heavenly Helpers will cover the role and duty of those who attained supernatural powers, to help others on Earth.

Part III: The Public Visitation Fairs has four chapters—Chapters 8 through 11:

Chapter 8: The Cyclical Renewal Festivals will cover the importance of holding and participating in annual festivals.

Chapter 9: Samples of Ancient-Present Festivals will cover about a dozen annual ancient Egyptian festivals and how many of them are very familiar and are being observed throughout the Western world.

Chapter 10: The Egyptian Spirited Fairs (Mouleds) will cover the main elements of a typical festival

Chapter 11: Egyptian Themes of Saint's Nick Traditional Festivities will offer a comparison between the commonly known Saint Nick's Christmas traditions and the typical Ancient Egyptian festival of a folk-saint.

Part IV: Come One Come All has two chapters—12 through 13.

Chapter 12: Fellowship Formations covers the general structure and practices to form/participate in a mystical fellowship.

Chapter 13: Isis —The Model Philosopher covers the principles and practices of Sufism as found in the Ancient Egyptian allegory of Isis and Osiris.

The contents of the three appendices are self evident from each's title, as follows:

Appendix A: Sleeping With the Enemy (Surviving Islam)

Appendix B: Zikr—The Ecstatic Practice

Appendix C: Reaching the Hearts and Minds (Effective Communication)

Moustafa Gadalla

3

PREFACE [1ST EDITION]

Herodotus stated, in 500 BCE: *"Of all the nations in the world, the Egyptians are the happiest, healthiest and most religious."*

Religiousness for the Ancient Egyptians was total cosmic consciousness. The Egyptian concept is now commonly known in the East as Sufism and in the West as alchemy.

This book explains how Ancient Egypt is the root of present-day Sufism/alchemy, and how the mystics of Egypt camouflaged their practices under a thin layer of Islam. This book will also show how other peoples tried to adopt the Egyptian model, but fell short and ended up with partial and incomplete applications. Egyptian mystical teachings and practices are markedly different from those practiced by Sufis in other countries, as is shown throughout this book.

The Egyptian model of mysticism is not about the outer world or a community of believers, dogma, scriptures, rules, or rituals. It does not involve simply believing that God is this, or God is that or that. It is not just asking one to "believe" and one is automatically in God's graces. The Egyptian model of mysticism consists of ideas and practices that provide the tools for any spiritual seeker to progress along each's alchemical Path towards "union with the Divine".

This spiritual Path towards union requires one to engage in the hard and sometimes painful (but joyful) commitment to inner and outer purification. The spiritual seeker must gain knowledge of reality/truth, do well in everything, and apply what he/she has learned in the world. It is a philosophy of life; a way of individual behavior in order to achieve the highest morality and internal happiness and peace.

The general perception of mysticism is that it is possible to achieve communion with God by attaining knowledge of spiritual truth through intuition acquired by fixed meditation. The Egyptian model for gaining knowledge is based on the utilization of both intellect and intuition.

In the Egyptian model, there are no "chosen people" who are picked by God or a religious authority. One must seek the Divine through a hard labor of love. Those who succeed in achieving union with the Divine are chosen and venerated by the masses.

This book intends to clarify these facts and to shed light on the Egyptian mystical model (Sufism)—yet not too much light; because that could endanger the traditions and their practitioners under the present ever-threatening dark cloud of Islam.

Moustafa Gadalla
To-beh 1, 13,001 (Ancient Egyptian Calendar)
January 9, 2003 CE

4

STANDARDS AND TERMINOLOGY

---

1. The Ancient Egyptian word neter and its feminine form, netert, have been wrongly and possibly intentionally translated to 'god' and 'goddess,' by almost all academicians. Neteru (plural of neter/netert) are the divine principles and functions of the One Supreme God.

2. You may find variations in writing the same Ancient Egyptian term, such as Amen/Amon/Amun or Pir/Per. This is because the vowels you see in translated Egyptian texts are only approximations of sounds which are used by Western Egyptologists to help them pronounce the Ancient Egyptian terms/words.

3. We will be using the most commonly recognized words for the English-speaking people that identify a neter/netert [god, goddess] or a pharaoh or a city; followed by other 'variations' of such a word/term.

It should be noted that the real names of the deities (gods, goddesses) were kept secret so as to guard the cosmic power of the deity. The Neteru were referred to by epithets that describe particular qualities, attributes and/or aspect(s) of their roles. Such applies to all common terms such as Isis, Osiris, Amun, Re, Horus, etc.

4. When using the Latin calendar, we will use the following terms:

BCE – Before Common Era. Also noted in other references as BC.
CE – Common Era. Also noted in other references as AD.

5. The term Baladi will be used throughout this book to denote the present silent majority of Egyptians that adhere to the Ancient Egyptian traditions, with a thin exterior layer of Islam.[See *Ancient Egyptian Culture Revealed,* by Moustafa Gadalla, for detailed information.]

6. There were/are no Ancient Egyptian writings/texts that were categorized by the Egyptians themselves as "religious", "funerary", "sacred", etc. Western academia gave the Ancient Egyptian texts arbitrary names, such as the "Book of This" and the "Book of That", "divisions", "utterances", "spells", etc. Western academia even decided that a certain "Book" had a "Theban version" or "this or that time period version". After believing their own inventive creation, academia then accused the Ancient Egyptians of making mistakes and missing portions of their writings(?!!).

For ease of reference, we will mention the common but arbitrary Western academic categorization of Ancient Egyptian texts, even though the Ancient Egyptians themselves never did.

MAP OF EGYPT AND SURROUNDING COUNTRIES

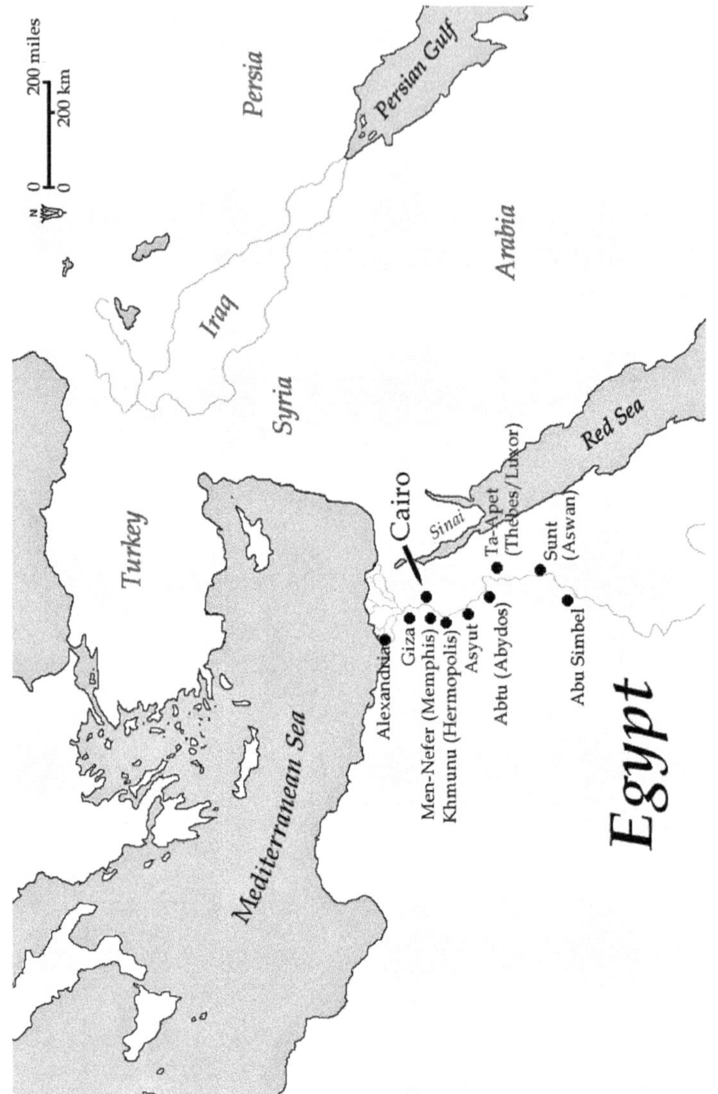

200 miles
200 km
N
Turkey
Syria
Iraq
Persia
Persian Gulf
Arabia
Mediterranean Sea
Red Sea
Sinai
Cairo
Alexandria
Giza
Men-Nefer (Memphis)
Khmunu (Hermopolis)
Asyut
Abtu (Abydos)
Ta-Apet
(Thebes/Luxor)
Sunt
(Aswan)
Abu Simbel
Egypt

PART I : THE HIDDEN TREASURE

Chapter 1 : Egyptian Mysticism and Islamized Sufism

1.1 DOGMATIC AND MYSTICAL ROUTES

Mankind is always trying to understand its own reason for existence relative to the universe in which it finds itself placed. There are generally two routes in which to search for the answers:

1. The dogmatic religions, whose basic assumption is that of a personal God who rules the universe and who communicates his will to man through prophets and lawgivers. This God is directly and personally concerned with the right ordering of this world, and with the right and righteous relationships he wishes to exist between man and man. Hence, he is the ultimate lawgiver. Christianity, Judaism, and Islam fall under this category.
2. The mystics, who do not believe in a personal God; for to call him God at all can only mislead. *He* is not a person and It is a principle—it is the principle of unchanging Being that is yet the source of all becoming; the stillness that is yet the source of all activity; and the One from which all multiplicity proceeds. This book will explain the Egyptian model of mysticism.

[For detailed information about source of creation, its cycle, and the governing universal powers, please read *Egyptian Cosmology:*

The animated Universe and *Egyptian Divinities: The All who are The One*; both by Moustafa Gadalla.]

1.2 EGYPTIANS: THE MOST RELIGIOUS

The Greek historian Herodotus (500 BCE) stated:

Of all the nations of the world, the Egyptians are the happiest, healthiest and most religious.

The excellent condition of the Egyptians was attributed to their application of metaphysical realities in their daily lives. In other words—total cosmic consciousness. 'As above so below' and 'as below so above' was the main law of existence for them—there was no perceived difference between sacred and mundane. Every action, no matter how mundane, was in some sense a cosmic corresponding act: plowing, sowing, reaping, brewing, playing games—all were viewed as earthly symbols for divine activities. The scenes of daily activities, found inside Egyptian tombs, show a strong perpetual correlation between the Earth and heavens.

In Egypt, what we now call religion was so widely acknowledged that it did not even need a name because it is life itself, in all its aspects. All their knowledge which was based on cosmic consciousness was embedded into their daily practices, which became traditions.

The mystical torch of the Ancient Egyptians has continued through the practices and traditions of the silent majority, Baladi Egyptians. Some of the Baladi Egyptians dedicate themselves to further spiritual enlightenment. These mystics of Egypt are called "Sufis" by others. Just like their ancestors, present-day Egyptian mystics dislike being given any inclusive name that might force them into doctrinal conformity. The Egyptian mystical seekers prefer to call themselves *Seekers of Ways*. Egyptian mysticism, now known as "Sufism", is (now) a name without reality. It once was a reality without a name. We only use the term 'mystics' or 'Sufis'. here, to identify them to readers.

A Seeker of the Way is anyone who believes that it is possible to have a direct experience of God and who seeks such a Path. The Egyptian model of mysticism is a natural expression of personal religion in relation to the expression of religion as a communal matter. It is an assertion of a person's right to seek contact with the source of being and reality as opposed to institutionalized religion, which is based on authority and a one-way Master-slave relationship, with its emphasis upon ritual observance and legalistic morality.

1.3 THE SOURCE OF SUFISM

The common premise is that "Sufism" is an Islamic group practicing a form of mysticism that originated in Persia.

As the book progresses, we will find that "Sufism" has nothing to do with Islam or Persia, and everything to do with the quiet peoples of Ancient and Baladi Egypt. Two points of interest should be mentioned here:

1. The term and practices of "Sufism" surfaced as a result of Islamic conquests and the subsequent terrorizing of its victims. In order for the Islamic-terrorized masses to maintain their ancient traditions, they had to camouflage old traditions under an Islamic garment.
2. The pure form of "Sufism" originated in Egypt. Other countries copied it and were quick to take the credit for it. Their application of "Sufism" is impure and incomplete, as we will find throughout this book.

The common premise (mentioned above) about the roots and essence of "Sufism" is absolutely wrong, as we will conclude by examining the facts throughout this book. Here are just a few introductory facts:

1. The notion of an Islamic origin of "Sufism" is wrong. "Islamic mysticism" is an oxymoron—as per the following selected points:

- The mystical seekers who are called "Sufis" have always suffered from Islamic rule throughout the ages. Many have been killed. They have been accused of attempting to make innovations on the dogmas of Islam; of following practices forbidden by the Koran; of denying the very existence of a personal Allah. The tolerance, or lack thereof, of Sufism in the Arabized/Islamized world is closely linked to the whim of the ruler and how he interprets/enforces Islamic laws. During certain periods, Sufism was/is tolerated; during others, it was outlawed and condemned.

- The keynote of mysticism (Sufism) is the union between man and God which, in Islam, is considered blasphemy; and as such is punishable by death by any Moslem, who is "empowered" to do so by the Koran itself!

- Islamic teachings are characterized by a consuming fear of God's wrath, while the Egyptian model of mysticism (Sufism) emphasizes love and not fear. God is perceived in terms of emotional closeness—"the friend," "the lover"—whose love can be experienced personally and individually.

- Mysticism (Sufism) is based on self-attained revelations by mystical means, which is contrary to Islam. Such revelations, as experienced by the mystical seekers (Sufis), are considered blasphemy and therefore are punishable by death, as established in the Koran.

- The Egyptian mystical seekers (Sufis) include in their ritual practices (as well as public festivals) specific methods to achieve ecstatic proximity to God through music, dance, or song. This runs contrary to Islam, where music, singing, and dancing are strictly forbidden, as clearly stated in all treatises on Islamic laws.

- Contrary to Islamic doctrine, Egyptian mysticism (Sufism)

bridges the gulf between man and God with folk saints. Veneration of folk saints and pilgrimages to their shrines represent an important aspect of the Egyptian Baladi mystical practices which is totally against the Islamic doctrine.

The above scene, from a stele dating about 4500 years ago, shows the Egyptian practices of veneration of folk saints, at their dome-roofed shrines, and presentations of offerings.

2. The claim of a Persian origin of "Sufism" is also wrong. The Persians themselves refer to Egypt as the source of "Sufism". For example:

a. The Egyptian Dhu 'l-Nun (died in 860 CE) is recognized in all Islamized Sufi references as the spiritual source of "Sufism" who prepared the way for the presently-known form of Islamized Sufism. Sufis claim him for their own as a leader and the originator of important concepts such as the mystic's direct knowledge (gnosis) of God and the stations and states of the spiritual Path. Dhu 'l-Nun was knowledge-able of the Ancient Egyptian hieroglyphs. A number of short treatises which deal with alchemy, magic, and medicine are attributed to him.

b. Thoth (Tehuti), the Ancient Egyptian **neter** (god), is recog-nized by all early (and later) Sufi writers as the ancient model of alchemy, mysticism, and all related subjects.

The well- known Sufi writer Idries Shah, who was an Iranian/Persian himself, admits the role of Egypt via Thoth and Dhu'I-Nun on Sufism and alchemy as follows:

> *. . . alchemical lore came from Egypt direct from the writings of Thoth . . . According to Sufi tradition the lore was transmitted through Dhu'i-Nun the Egyptian, the King or Lord of the Fish, one of the most famous of classical Sufi teachers.* [The Sufis, 1964]

Thoth's name appears among the ancient masters of what is now called the Way of the Sufis. In other words, both the Sufis and the alchemists recognize Tehuti as the foundation of their knowledge.

Idries Shah also makes a direct reference to the Spanish-Arab historian Said of Toledo (who died in 1069) who outlines this tradition of the Ancient Egyptian Thoth (aka Hermes):

> *Sages affirm that all antediluvian sciences originate with the Egyptian Hermes [Thoth], in Upper Egypt. The Jews call him Enoch and the Moslems Idris. He was the first who spoke of the material of the superior world and of planetary movements . . . Medicine and poetry were his functions . . . [as well as] the sciences, including alchemy and magic.* [Cf. Asin Palacios, Ibn Masarra, p. 13]

c. It is an indisputable fact that all Sufi mystical terms are not Persian (or Turkish). All Sufi terms are "Arabic". The "Arabic" language is substantially of Egyptian origin. After the Arab/Islamic conquests of their neighboring countries (including Egypt), they simply cancelled the identity of their victimized countries,= and labeled them "Arabs".

3. To continue the point above (regarding the language of Sufism), it should be noted that the word Sufi was never mentioned in the Koran or in Mohammed's sayings. There is no consensus on its meaning. The "translation" of the word/term "Sufi" as a "wearer of wool" is totally fabricated, and is one of many attempted explanations.

The word is actually of Ancient Egyptian origin. **Seph/Soph** was a component of common Egyptian names; meaning wisdom and purity (among many other meanings).

4. Some of the standard Sufi terms that are often used are: *old religion, antique faith, old one,* and *ancient tradition*. Such terms were used/stressed by all early Sufi writers, which is indicative of the pre-Islamic origins of Sufism.

5. The Egyptians are remarkable traditionalists to a fault. Early historians have attested to this fact, such as: Herodotus, in *The Histories, Book Two*, 79:

> **The Egyptians keep to their native customs and never adopt any from abroad.**

And Herodotus in *The Histories, Book Two*, 91:

> **The Egyptians are unwilling to adopt Greek customs, or, to speak generally, those of any other country.**

Plato and other writers affirmed the complete adherence of the Egyptians to their own traditions.

6. Supernatural powers acclaimed by the mystics (Sufis) are often called *magic*. From the earliest times, Egypt has been celebrated for its magicians, and accounts of their marvelous achievements have been documented not only in Ancient Egyptian records, but also in the Bible and in the works of several classical writers. Furthermore, many of the tales in the famous collection of stories known as *The Arabian Nights* show what wonder-working powers were attributed to magicians in medieval Egypt.

Heka [shown above] represents the Ancient Egyptian magical power of words. He is usually depicted holding two snakes with total ease.

7. The country that has the largest number of "Sufi" followers is Egypt. Participation in Sufi fellowships (orders) in other countries besides Egypt is very small in comparison.

Egyptian mysticism (Sufism) is not an offshoot of Islam; it is the old "religion" camouflaged into Arabized/Islamized terms.

Egyptian mystical seekers (Sufis) maintain low profiles, for they seek no public glory; but rather the ultimate mystical glory—The Divine.

Chapter 2 : The Treasure Within

2.1 THE IMAGE OF GOD

Egyptian mysticism's (and likewise, Sufism's) main keynote is the union—the identification of God and man.

It is commonly recognized by all theological and philosophical schools of thought that human beings are made in the image of God – i.e. a miniature universe – and that to understand the universe is to understand oneself, and vice versa.

Yet, no culture has ever practiced the above principle like the Ancient Egyptians. Central to their complete understanding of the universe was the knowledge that man was made in the image of God and, as such, man represented the image of all creation. Accordingly, Egyptian symbolism has always related to man.

When we ask "Who is God?", we are really asking: "*What* is God?". One can only define "God" through the multitude of "His" attributes/qualities/powers actions. To know God is to know the numerous qualities of God. In other words, the more we understand of the multiplicity of his actions, attributes, etc., the more we realize the totality of the One—The Unity of Multiplicity. Far from being a primitive, polytheistic form, this is the highest expression of monotheistic mysticism.

The concept of Egyptian monotheism can also apply to man—the image of God. If we refer to, say, a person as Mr. X, it means nothing to us. However, we begin to learn/know more of Mr.

X when we learn of his attributes, qualities, actions, deeds, etc. A person who is an engineer, a father, a husband, etc. does not have polypersonalities; but rather a mono-personality with multiple functions/attributes. Man is the perfect example of Unity of Multiplicity.

Within each human being is a "treasure", and this can be found only by looking for it. The Egyptian model of mysticism unleashes the inner hidden potential of the human being to learn, gain knowledge, and achieve.

2.2 ORGANS OF PERCEPTION

Human faculties, although perceptive, are limited—like a radio that can receive only certain electro-magnetic waves and not other parts of the band. The perceived world is therefore a distortion. The inability to transcend the barrier of our limited senses explains human shortcomings in understanding the complete reality of the world around us, in all its aspects.

The flaw in Western culture is the inflation of the intellect at the expense of intuitive knowledge. This is one-dimensional thinking, which distorts the understanding of reality because it blocks other modes of consciousness.

The Egyptian mystics distinguish between the ordinary knowing of fact and the inner knowing of reality. Their activities connect and balance all these factors—understanding, being, and knowing. The Egyptian mystical goal is to establish equilibrium between the intellect and the inner faculties so that, instead of canceling each other, they interact and enrich one another. Therefore, the Egyptian mystics develop their intuitive modes of consciousness to counterbalance the rational mode. The goal is to achieve equilibrium between rational and non-rational modes of consciousness.

The main Egyptian mystical (Sufi) theme is the importance of consciousness in integrating inner faculties into comprehension through a gradual process. The Egyptian mystics refer to this process as using all organs of perception for a more comprehensive understanding.

Uniting/balancing and integrating complimentary opposites is one of the main and constant themes in Ancient Egypt. [More about this process in Chapter 6.]

2.3 THE POWER OF LOVE

For a person to excel in anything, one must love what one is doing. Love conquers all. Love makes everything easy. For the sake of reaching a goal, the lover feels no pain, struggle, obstacles, sacrifice, etc. towards their goal. Sufis call themselves truth seekers and truth lovers, which is reminiscent of the Ancient Egyptian Ma-at (representing the truth) lovers and seekers that permeate Ancient Egyptian texts. [More about Ma-at later on.]

The Egyptian mystical seeker is a philosopher in the original meaning of the term (philo = love, sophy = truth).

To love the truth is to love the whole truth and nothing but the truth—no matter what the consequences are.

But love to the Egyptian mystical seeker (Sufi) means action, not merely enjoyment or even the despair of one-sided love. Love is the most powerful motivation, and must be both active and passive. Active love leads to seeking, action, determination, endurance, etc. The passive form of love is total surrender in order to receive, learn, and absorb.

Man's love towards the Divine is a quality that manifests itself in the heart of the Divine seeker in the form of veneration and magnification so that he seeks to satisfy his Beloved and becomes impatient and restless in his desire for visions of Him, and cannot rest with anyone except Him. Love means attraction and being drawn to your Beloved—it's as powerful as a magnet. This powerful emotion/motivation is described as being crazy for/about the Beloved. Love is adoration, devotion, affection, passion, endearment and yearning. The yearning aspect of love is one of the most motivating forces in the whole journey of the return to the Divine Origin.

The goal of the Egyptian mystical seeker is to remove all the veils between himself/herself and God. The final veil is the "I"—the sense of separateness that we each carry. The philosophers (truth lovers) seek a similar path of love towards the Divine. For them, the goal is for the beloved, lover, and love to reunite—to become One.

With the power of love, the mystical aspirant can seek the Divine through self-transformation.

PART II :
TRANSFORMATION FROM DUST TO GOLD

Chapter 3 : The Alchemist Way

3.1 ATUM/ADAM: THE ALCHEMIST GOAL

In Judaism, Christianity, and Islam, Adam is considered to be the first human being. In Sufi traditions, Adam symbolizes the "Perfect Person (Man)". The above-mentioned common beliefs are of Ancient Egyptian origin, as follows:

> 1. When the name Adam is written in the equivalent Ancient Egyptian alphabetical characters, it becomes *Atam/Atum*. In Ancient Egyptian traditions, *Atam/Atum* represents the first realization of existence.

> 2. Atam/Atum means *he who completes* or *perfects*. In other words, *Atam* represents the Perfect Person. *Atam/Atum*, in the Litany of *Ra*, is recognized as the ALL.

In the *Unas Funerary* (so-called Pyramid) *Texts*, there is the following invocation:

> **Salutation to thee, Atam, . . . Thou art high in this thy name High Mound, . . . [§1587]**

The high mound where Adam/*Atam/Atum* stands is the Ancient Egyptian Ben stone, known in Sufi traditions as the *Philosopher's Stone* or the *Alchemist Stone*—the agent believed to transmute baser metals into gold and to prolong life indefinitely. This alchemist/Sufi tradition of transforming matter (**Ben**) into gold

(**Neb**) is of an Ancient Egyptian origin, as reflected in their language as follows:

- **Ben** has several related meanings: *the primordial stone, the mound of creation, the first state of matter, opposition/negation, it is not, there is not, multiplicity.*
- The mirror image of Ben is **Neb** (**Ben** spelled backwards), which also has several related meanings: *gold* (traditionally the finished perfected end product—the goal of the alchemist), *lord, master, all, affirmation, pure.*

This **Ben** and **Neb** mirror image mode/theme permeated Ancient Egyptian thinking and was later adopted into the Islamized Sufi traditions in the following ideas:

- the metaphor of the mirror
- reality and image (God and Man)
- the metaphor of the broken pieces
- the concept of duality
- reversing the Path from/to God is a mirror image (**Ben** to **Neb**). [See a later chapter for more details about all the above points.]

The transformation from **Ben** (matter) to **Neb** (gold) is analogous to the alchemist traditions, which draw parallels between metal and spiritual purification.

The Ancient Egyptian alchemical knowledge was, according to Sufi traditions, transmitted through Dhu'iNun the Egyptian (who died in 860 CE), from the ThriceGreat Thoth (aka Tehuti, Hermes) as the reputed originator of alchemy, and by all Islamized Sufi sources. His name appears among the ancient masters of what is now called the Way of the Sufis.

3.2 PROGRESSIVE SOWING AND REAPING

The progress of the spiritual life is described as a journey or a pilgrimage consisting of slow progressions toward the goal of union with Reality. The Path/Way is a practical method to guide a mystical seeker through a succession of "stages" toward the ultimate goal of unification with the Divine. The "stages" of the journey have been variously described in the Islamized Sufi traditions as consisting of 7, 10, etc. stages. Such progressive stages are clearly described in the countless Ancient Egyptian transformational (funerary) texts detailing the journey of the successful soul from its earthly living towards the Divine.

Each "stage" of the Path is acquired through striving, and is a matter of conscious, disciplined action. Whenever an aspirant achieves a certain level of personal development, he is rewarded psychologically, with certain spiritual liberation. As such, the Path/Way consists of spiritual stations and corresponding spiritual states. Stages are steps taken by us—rising/ascending. The "states" form a similar psychological chain. The experiences of the spiritual states feel like liberations/releases that descend into one's heart. That sense of relief is equivalent to untying the knots—a problem/question has been resolved. Such experience will elevate the mystical seeker to a higher level, where he/she can continue to learn, using both intellect and intuition.

3.3 YOUR GUIDING ANGELS

In order for the Egyptian mystical seeker to attain his goal and reach the end of his journey, he is advised to follow the directions of a leader who lays down for him certain rules of practice and guides him in every detail of his life. It is much easier to have a spiritual guide in the earlier stages of spiritual development because there is a human tendency to overlook our own obstacles—to ignore them or deny their existence even when we have seen them clearly. Therefore, it is difficult for us to achieve and sustain spiritual clarity without someone other than ourselves leading us beyond our own shortcomings. As such, it is understood that at some point in your development, you will need to work with a guide/coach which is known in strict Islamized countries as *sheikh* (the same term for Islamic clergy).

The guide assists the mystical aspirants in moving closer to realizing their inner nature. By helping us to reconnect with our own inner wisdom, the guide empowers and enables us to continue the pilgrimage back to ourselves.

The guide teaches out of his or her own personal understanding and fullness of being. The guide is someone who has successfully passed the first two stages of purification and attainment of knowledge [as explained later on]. The guide's role consists of a combination of a guide/coach/ teacher/soulmate/friend/pilot/ navigator/spiritual medium. There are a variety of guides with different capabilities. In larger mystic (Sufi) fellowships (orders), there are usually several guides who work as a "coaching" team to guide the mystical aspirant through his spiritual progression. The most prominent functions of the guide are:

1. **As a guide**, he shows the way—but the aspirant must himself do the walking. Man must develop by his own effort toward growth of an evolutionary nature, stabilizing his consciousness. The guide leads his disciple from the beginning of his journey to its end, guiding him at every 'stage' and helping him in every 'state'.

2. **As a friend**, he is a companion and adviser who provides reassurance and a point of view that is influenced by his perception of the other's need.

3. **As a soulmate**, he establishes a relationship and means of communication between himself and the mystical seeker that transcends the conventional relationship between a teacher and a learner, since a part of the teaching and learning stands outside time and space. The process of learning depends on the degree of reciprocity of the candidate through his experience with the teacher and not on an argu-

mentative basis. The guide, as such, is more than just one who passes on formal knowledge. As such, the relationship between them is formed as an affectionate bond in which spiritual support and protection are maintained.

4. **As a spiritual medium**, he connects (through the spiritual lineage of a fellowship) with the founder of the mystic fellowship, Pir/Mir/Wali. This founder is the person who, while alive on earth, has achieved all three levels of consciousness [as explained later on], and thus became/becomes a permanent power in the higher realms. In other words, the Pir/Mir/Wali is the completed human being from whom the particular mystical (Sufi) fellowship derives its Bara-ka (spiritual powers). The guide, through his spiritual training and attainment, is able to 'transmit' spiritual power from the founder-Pir to his mystical aspirants.

It should be noted that both the mystical seekers and their guides have their own incomes, and their relationship is void of any financial exchange. [More about the role of the guide and the spiritual chain/lineage throughout this book.]

3.4 ANUBIS—ARCHETYPAL ALCHEMICAL GUIDE

In our return to our divine origin, we each need a guide/ guiding angel that we can trust to lead us in the right direction. This Path Finder is symbolized by the dog Anubis, who represents the right sense of direction—the Divine Guide.

We will summerize Anubis' functions as:

- The Path Finder
- The Alchemist Diet
- The Truth Finder

Anubis the dog is the divine guide for the dog is known for his homing instinct day or night.

The metaphysical role of Anubis the dog is reflected in his diet. The dog/jackal feasts on carrion, turning it into beneficial nourishment. In other words, Anubis represents the capacity to turn waste into useful food for the body (and soul)—as in the alchemical way—transforming lead into gold.

An absolute sense of loyalty is embodied into the dog.

Anubis represents the right sense of direction in whatever we do; the absolute loyalty and the capacity to turn lead (carrion) into gold (worthiness).

Anubis also represents the Truth Finder. In the Isis/Osiris allegory, it is Anubis that helps Isis find the scattered pieces of Osiris as the *Manifester of the Truth.*

To find the broken pieces so as to bind them together is the essence of *Religion.* The origin of the word Re-ligio-n is the word *Religio,* which means *to bind together.*

3.5 THE THRICE THOTH

In Ancient Egyptian traditions, the words of Ra (Re), revealed through Thoth, became the things and creatures of this world; i.e. the words (meaning sound energies) created the forms in the universe. As such, Thoth represents the link between the metaphysical (extra-human) and the physical (terrestrial).

Early Islamized Sufi traditions describe Thoth of Egypt as the neter (god) who:

- Was the link between the extra-human and the terrestrial.

- Like the aspiring mystic, Thoth is represented as a bird. Sometimes he is a man with the head of an ibis, where the head would indicate aspiration or attainment in the mind, localized in the head.

- Moved, like Mercury (his equivalent), at immense speed, negating time and space in the same way that inner experience does.

- Is an athlete; a developed man.

- Is shown as a mature man; a man of age and wisdom. As such, Thoth is associated with a form of wisdom that is transmitted to man from divine sources.

- Created the lyre with three strings and, through its music, aroused in the hearers three levels of consciousness. Thoth's music is the means of transmission and intermediation between human and divine. [More about this item throughout the book under the name **Samaa**.]

Thoth is commonly known as Thrice Thoth, representing the three levels of consciousness. A new/raised consciousness is equivalent to a new awakening. In Sufi traditions, each of the three levels of consciousness are referred to as death—rebirth. The same thinking has pervaded Ancient (and present-day)

Egypt, where birth and rebirth is a constant theme. The word 'death' is employed in a figurative sense. The theme that man must "die before he dies" or that he must be "born again" in his present life is taken symbolically, or is commemorated by a ritual. In this, the candidate has to pass through certain specific experiences (technically termed "deaths"). A good example is baptism, which was the main objective at Easter, after Lent, representing death of the old self by immersing into water, and the rising of the new/renewed self by coming out of the water.

The three levels of consciousness in the Egyptian mystical traditions are:

1. The purification process of body and soul.

2. Gaining knowledge through both intellect and intuition (revelation). The objective, in simple terms, is to put the pieces of the cosmic puzzle together, but the lines separating the pieces are still visible.

3. Vanishment into the Divine Essence through the cessation of all conscious thought. In the puzzle metaphor, it is when the puzzle is complete, and the mystic no longer sees the lines between the pieces.

The mystical seeker must succeed in each of these levels before advancing to the next higher level.

Chapter 4 : The Purification Process

4.1 PURE GOLD (PURIFYING THE HEART AND TONGUE)

The Ancient Egyptian transformational (funerary) texts are permeated with purity as a prerequisite for advancing to higher realms/heavens. The Egyptian model of mysticism stresses that purity can only be achieved through purifying the heart and practicing pure intent in ordinary daily life.

In the Ancient Egyptian traditions, the active faculties of Atum/Atam/Adam (The Perfect Man) were intelligence, which was identified with the heart and identified as Horus—a solar neter (god) – and action, which was identified with the tongue and identified as Thoth—a lunar neter (god). The solar and lunar neteru (gods) stress his universal character. In the Shabaka Stele (dated from the 8th century BCE, but it is a reproduction of a 3rd Dynasty text), we read:

> *There came into being as the heart (Horus), and there came into being as the tongue (Thoth), the form of Atam.*

One thinks with the heart and acts with the tongue, as described on the Shabaka Stele:

> *The Heart thinks all that it wishes, and the Tongue delivers all that it wishes.*

The significance of heart and tongue permeates Ancient Egyptian texts and was subsequently adopted in "Sufism".

The Ancient Egyptian depiction shows the Perfected Person being purified by the combined action of his heart (Horus) and tongue (Thoth), with water in the forms of the ankh and the was, which represents the lustral water. The ankh represents eternal life, and the was represents authority; i.e. total self-control.

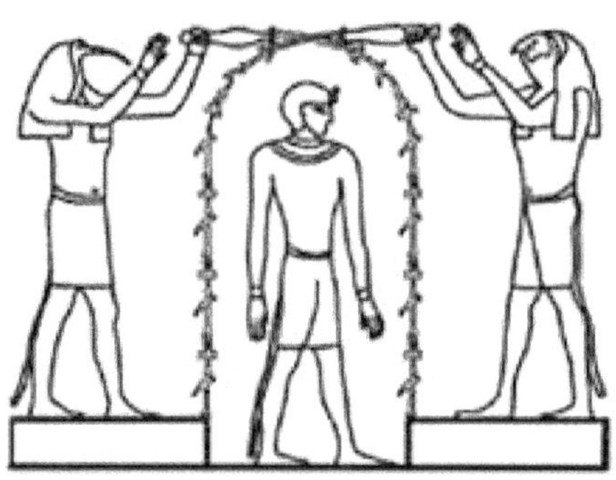

Likewise, the aspirant, in the Egyptian model, learns to purify his inner self by taming vices and practicing the opposites of such vices in society. Knowledge is both gained by the mind and acquired by experience. Inner purification must be completed by practicing good social behavior in ordinary daily life. Every action impresses itself upon the heart. The inward being of a person is really the reflection of his deeds and actions. Doing good deeds thus establishes good inner qualities and the virtues impressed upon the heart in turn govern the actions of the limbs. As each act, thought, and deed makes an image on the heart, it becomes an attribute of the person. This maturation of the soul through acquired attributes leads to progressive mystical visions and an ultimate unification with the Divine.

Reciprocally, the knowledge obtained by both intellect and intuition is a source of virtue that must be practiced in ordinary life. The struggle for virtue and the vision of the Divine are all aspects of a single progressive achievement in the course of which the aspirant becomes wiser, until he achieves the totality of being that simultaneously entails mystical vision and ordinary piety.

4.2 THE HEALTHY BODY

In our present times, we say "Cleanliness is next to Godliness," and "Your body is a temple." These premises have always been the view of the mystical Egyptians.

To have a healthy mind and spirit, one must have a healthy body and surroundings. In their conceptions of moral purity, the Ancient Egyptians always emphasized sanitary observances of the human body and surroundings.

The most sacred of Ancient Egyptian texts, such as the *Book of Coming Forth by Light* (commonly known as the *Book of the Dead*), emphasize:

- Maintaining a clean body, such as frequent bathing, mouth washing, clipping and cleaning fingernails and toenails, shaving (including body hair), washing hands and feet, etc.

- Purity of the food. Herodotus (500 BCE) describes the measures taken by the Egyptians to ensure the ceremonial purity of sacrificial animals.

The ancient traditions emphasize maintaining good eating habits with an attitude of eat to live—not live to eat. They also recommend going through cyclical internal cleansing by fasting (abstention from eating fish, meat, and dairy products for a cycle of 40 days) and other means.

Exercises and staying in shape were/are essential for the Ancient and the mystical Baladi Egyptians. The Ancient Egyptian King was not supposed (or even able) to reign unless he was in good health and spirit. The Pharaoh was required to run a 5-mile (8 km) course in the annual Heb-Sed rituals.

A healthy and clean body is a prerequisite to all daily activities, in the Egyptian model of mystical seeking.

4.3 GETTING OUT OF THE BOX

It is commonly understood that the figure of a cubical box represents the restraint of human potential.

The Egyptian was highly conscious of the box-like structure, which is the model of the Earth or the material world. This form of statuary, called the "cube statue", is prevalent since the Middle Kingdom (2040-1783 BCE). The subject was integrated into the cubic form of the stone. In these cube statues, there is a powerful sense of the subject emerging from the confinement of the cube. Its symbolic significance is that the spiritual principle is emerging from the material world. The earthly person is placed unmistakably in material existence.

Cultivation of the desired virtues has the effect of liberating the aspirant from the material world by emerging from the box—the lower self.

The Divine person is shown sitting squarely on a cube; i.e. mind over matter.

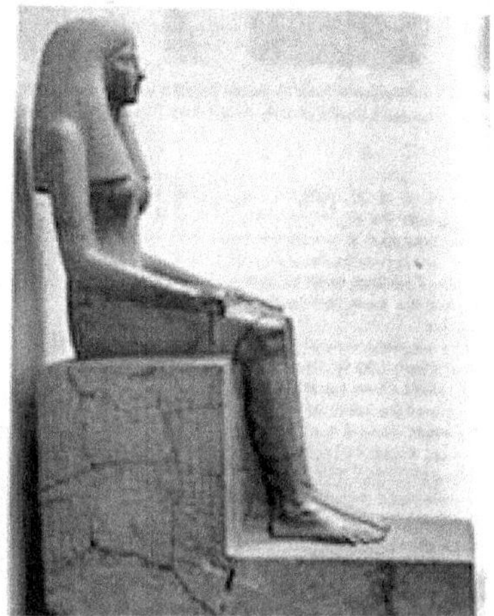

Other traditions, such as the Platonic and Pythagorean, adopted the same concept of the Egyptian cubic representation of the material world.

4.4 BATTLING THE ENEMIES (IMPURITIES) WITHIN

There are basically two forces within each of us: one pulling us down into the box and the other pulling us out of the box. This archetypal inner struggle in the Egyptian model is symbolized in the struggle between Horus and Seth. It is the archetypal struggle between opposing forces. Horus, in this context, is the divine man, born of nature, who must do battle against Seth, his own kin, representing the power of opposition (and not evil in the narrow sense). Seth represents the concept of opposition in all aspects of life (physically and metaphysically).

We must continuously learn and evolve, like Horus, whose name means *He Who is Above*. In other words, we must strive to reach higher and higher. We learn and act by affirmation of the Horus in each of us, and by negating the Seth within us. The obstacles within each of us, represented by Seth, must be controlled and/or overcome.

In Ancient Egyptian temples, tombs, and texts, human vices are depicted as foreigners (the sick body is sick because it is/was invaded by foreign germs). Foreigners are depicted as subdued—arms tightened/tied behind their backs—to portray inner self-control. The most vivid example of self-control is the common depiction of the Pharaoh (The Perfected Man) on the outer walls of Ancient Egyptian temples, subduing/controlling foreign enemies—the enemies (impurities) within.

To battle the enemies within, we must identify and acknowledge each of them. Stories and other means of expression personify bad manners such as arrogance, anger, envy, etc. The characters in the Egyptian stories will help you see these impurities in yourself (mirror image) so you can hate, reject, and defeat them. Other forms of expression, such as proverbs and humor, serve the same purpose.

We need to identify and control/cleanse the impurities within ourselves, which impede our judgment and ultimate objective.

4.5 THE EGO—PERSONAL ENEMY #1

The supreme obstacle for the human being is his own egotistic consciousness that is dominated by pride, egotism, self-centered greed, and lust.

Controlling the ego was/is one of the most important ethical requirements in the Egyptian model of mysticism. One of the Egyptian King's titles was *The Most Humble*. His abode while on Earth was made of mud-brick—the same material used by the humblest peasants.

To cultivate humility, the mystical aspirant must consider himself a servant. Aspirants practice humility by serving others without exception. The richest and most educated of the Egyptian mystics (Sufis) are found begging on street corners, serving water to the public, cleaning bathrooms, etc.

The Ancient Egyptian transformational (funerary) texts show that one must overcome many obstacles on the way towards the ultimate reunification. The main obstacle is the ego. To reunite with the Divine, we must be ego-free.

This symbolic Ancient Egyptian scene [shown above] depicts Horus and his four disciples (sons), each armed with a knife, demonstrating to Osiris their success in controlling the ego. Their success is symbolized by the ass-headed man (symbol of the ego in man) with knives stuck in his body, bound by his arms to the forked stick.

In an Ancient Egyptian Instruction given in 2380 BCE to a soon-to-be high official, the words begin as follows:

Do not be arrogant because you are learned; do not be over-confident because you are we well informed; Consult the ignorant man as well as the wise one.

There is a significant difference between the Egyptian mystical (Sufi) model and that of the Asian versions of Sufism—in particular, the Persian version. While humility is the paramount feature of Egyptian teachings, other versions are the exact opposite. While Egyptians don't associate their extensive wisdom texts with individuals, the Persians love to brag, describing their "writers" as "incomparable", "incredible", and "inimitable" in the titles of their "booklets", such as:

The Exploits of the Incomparable Mulla Nasrudin
The Pleasantries of the Incredible Mulla Nasrudin
The Subtleties of the Inimitable Mulla Nasrudin

It should come as no surprise that these and other similar "unhumble" titles are totally void of wisdom; for humility is a pre-requisite to wisdom.

4.6 THE DO'S AND DON'TS

To achieve inner purification, one must cultivate good manners (affirmation) and suppress bodily impulses (negations). Inner purification can only be achieved through both learning and practicing [as explained earlier].

Ancient Egyptian wisdom has always laid great emphasis on the cultivation of ethical behavior and service to society. The constant theme of the Egyptian wisdom literature was the 'acting out' of Truth—**Maa Kheru**—on Earth.

Ma-at represents the truth; the Way. She is always depicted wearing the feather of truth on her head. Likewise, the Sufis speak of the Path/Way, and seeking the truth. In Ancient Egypt, the concept of **Ma-at** has permeated all Egyptian writings, from the earliest times and throughout Egyptian history. **Ma-at**, The Way, encompasses the virtues, goals, and duties that define acceptable (if not ideal) social interaction and personal behavior. **Ma-at** is maintained in the world by the correct actions and personal piety of its adherents.

A summary of the Egyptian conception of righteousness can be found in what is popularly known as the Negative Confessions. A more detailed picture of a righteous man and the expected conduct and the ideas of responsibility and retribution can be obtained from the walls of tomb chapels and in several literary compositions that are usually called 'wisdom texts'. Among them are the 30 chapters of *The Teaching of Amenemope,* which contain collections of poetic phrases of moral content and advice. Such teachings were later copied in the *Old Testament's Book of Proverbs.*

In addition to the different modes of learning [as referred to in Appendix D], there were additional practical wisdom texts of systematic instructions, composed of maxims and precepts. [See *Egyptian Cosmology: The Animated Universe* by this same author for samples.]

To be liberated from one's box, the mystical aspirant must look himself/herself in the mirror, so to speak, and must both negate (refrain) vices and affirm (cultivate) virtues. For example:

1. Refrain from such vices as: envy, backbiting. Purge ignorance, uncharitableness, the ego, laziness, over-confidence, arrogance, evasiveness, indifference, gluttony, vices of speech, anger, hypocrisy, conceit, etc.

2. Cultivate virtues such as:

    – The recognition of a fault and ensuring that it will never happen again. (repentance)
    – Fortitude and gratitude.
    – Single-hearted devotion, love, yearning/longing.
    – Resolve, truthfulness.
    – Contemplation, self-examination, and self-evaluation.
    – Patience.
    – Silence and listening.
    – Hunger for knowledge.
    – Humility.
    – Satisfaction/contentment.

– Servanthood.
– Willpower/determination.
– Righteousness by following the straight path.
– Sincerity.

We must continuously critique ourselves. We must continue to contemplate, evaluate, act, and re-examine ... over and over again.

4.7 THE PAUPER IS A PRINCE

To be liberated from the box, the aspirant must reject the confinement of the material world. Material wealth must not be the goal of the mystical aspirant. In the Egyptian model, the mystical aspirant must work, but must not be enslaved in compiling wealth. Being wealthy is fine, as long as becoming wealthy is not the main objective. The Egyptian mystic ideal of materialistic poverty is a lack of desire for wealth. The ascending reward for material apathy is the feeling of contentment and peace of mind. It is a sort of liberation from the box—the material world.

One must be full of bountifulness and generosity; i.e. give back of yourself, time, money, etc. Material apathy means living a simple, moderate life—not going to extremes.

In the unique Egyptian mystical model, humility of spirit and demeanor are required from all. They are taught not to consider themselves superior to others, but to rank themselves as among the poorest, lowest, and most humble of mankind. It is therefore that these mystics are distinguished by the deep humility of their manner. Their heads are ever bent; their gazes absorbed. As a result, they have tolerance and goodwill towards all mankind, irrespective of race or creed.

Once the person is pure (of body, mind, and spirit), the aspirant has succeeded in reaching the first level of consciousness.

The second level involves gaining knowledge through both intellect and spiritual experience (revelation). At this time, the aspirant must join (if he did not join earlier) a mystic fellowship compatible with his personality in order to find a spiritual guide and to participate in group activities.

Chapter 5 : Basic Practices

The first stage of purification is vastly improved by performing/ following special practices. These practices become essential for advancement in the second and third (final) stages of the Spiritual Path.

5.1 THE POWER OF CONCENTRATION

The achievement of the balance between the 'physical' world and the inner levels of perception is essential. The difficulty lies in retaining it, since this balance is connected with the fact that ordinary humanity is not able (except for very short periods) to concentrate at all. The process of retaining that balance in the memory takes place in stages referred to by the Egyptian mystics as 'states and stations', as mentioned in an earlier chapter.

Concentration is also necessary for serious contemplation (thoughtful inspection/study). It is the only way to put things together. The more (and deeper) the aspirant concentrates, the more expansive his horizon becomes. Therefore, exercises to improve concentration are essential for the mystical seeker. Some basic exercises used by the mystical seekers include: playing games, juggling, sports, board games, musical training, whirling, etc.

Concentration skills are also beneficial in all other practices/ activities, such as breathing, playing music, etc.

Advanced concentration practices must be performed under strict supervision by qualified guides. Such practices without supervision are harmful and possibly dangerous.

5.2 THE ANIMATED BREATHING TECHNIQUES

The term *breath* has special significance to the Egyptian mystic because it resonates on both the physical and spiritual levels. The *breath of life* is known in Ancient Egypt as Amen/Amon/Amun. He represents the hidden or occult force underlying creation. The Ancient Egyptian papyrus known as the Leiden Papyrus describes Amen as:

> **He [who] gives birth to everything that is and causes all that exists to live.**

In the Egyptian mystical traditions, learning breathing rhythms is essential in the ecstatic practice known as *zikr*, which involves controlled breathing rhythms, dancing, and the chanting of musical compositions.

The Egyptian mystic learns to breathe properly. The natural breathing rhythm is reflected in the binary and ternary method of time measurement in musical performance. When a person is in a quiet sleep, the time between expiration and inhalation is twice as long as that between inhalation and exhalation. The underlying binary or ternary rhythm is known as the fundamental rhythm. Subdivisions of these beats that appear within the general musical framework are called the subsidiary rhythm.

Breathing practices must be taught and supervised by qualified mystical guides.

5.3 PLAYING MUSIC

Concentration and breathing techniques are taught and practiced by Egyptian mystics (Sufis) while they learn to play musical instruments—especially wind instruments such as the end-blown reed pipe (nay) and mizmar (double clarinets). The Egyptian nay player led, and continues to lead, all religious processions in both Ancient and present-day festivals.

Post-Islam mysticism (Sufism) traditions acknowledge that appropriate music is the means of transmission and intermediation between human and Divine, known as *'samaa'*. The godfather of post-Islam mysticism (Sufism), namely the Egyptian Dhu-'I-Nun el-Massri, said, of *'samaa'*:

> *"Those who listen with their souls can hear the heavenly music/call.":*

The famed Sufi Al-Ghazali (who spent years in Egypt) introduced music into the Sufi rites based on Ancient Egyptian practices which were introduced by Dhu-'INun, the Egyptian. He makes the following statement:

> *"The Sufis, most venerated for their sanctity and doctrine, like Dhu-'I-Nun the Egyptian, had no scruples about the use of music as an important element in religious practices of ascetic life."*

Playing other musical instruments are also important, such as double reed-pipes, tri-kanun (zithers), shortnecked lutes (oud), kamangas (violins), horns, clappers, cymbals, castanets, small drums, and tambourines. Music plays an important role in ancient and present-day practices and festivals, as will be detailed later in this book.

5.4 RECITATIONS OF NAMES, ROSARIES, ETC.

To achieve higher concentration, Egyptian mystics guide their disciples through a graduated series of different forms of ejaculatory prayers, performed for daily recitation chiefly with the help of a rosary. Egyptian beads were always an important part of their rituals, for over 5,000 years.

Recitations consist of repeating a word, name, or a phrase, numerous times. This is reminiscent of the Ancient Egyptians' *Litany of Re*. The Litany begins with a brief preface and then is followed by 75 invocations to the names/forms of Re, followed by a series of prayers and hymns. Each recited name represents a specific aspect/attribute of Re.

The Ancient Egyptian texts provide an extensive number and variety of litanies, rosaries, eulogies, psalms, hymns, etc. Likewise, present-day Egyptian mystics (Sufis) utilize the same ancient poetic and recitative compositions.

Egyptian mystics have a countless number of these poetic and musical compositions that they know by heart. Each composition is sung/recited at a specific time and on specific occasions. These hundreds of Egyptian compositions are too old to be accredited to specific authors.

Recitation of names and rosaries are important in the ecstatic practice of **zikr**. The mystical rosaries (awrad) are usually a long, well-composed series in the form of poetic stanzas or recitations. Each rosary consists of well-designed components/sections, each with its own particular climaxes. These rosaries are replete with wise proverbial sayings, pious reflections, and moral precepts. The leader of the **zikr** chooses (and frequently modifies) the rosaries required for each practice to fit the event, the level of participants, etc. [See the next chapter and other parts of the book for details about the **zikr**.]

5.5 SPORTS AND RHYTHMIC MOVEMENTS

Maintaining a healthy athletic body was/is essential in the Egyptian model. Such perfect conditioning is attributed to the Patron of Alchemy—Thoth. Diodorus, in *Book I* (16), wrote:

> *It was by Thoth, for instance, according to the Egyptians, that . . .he was the first . . .to establish a wrestling school, and to give thought to the rhythmical movement of the human body and its proper development. . . .*

Wrestling [as shown below, from an Ancient Egyptian tomb] is one of the many sports that is practiced by present-day mystical seekers (Sufis).

Rhythmic movements/exercises/games that are practiced by the mystical seekers include, but are not limited to: yoga, martial arts, wrestling, etc. A unique Egyptian rhythmic ritual/game is the performing of routines with wooden swords [as shown below]. This is a very ritualistic and graceful game that requires immense concentration and talent.

The benefits of sports is very important in the life of the mystic, since it combines the benefit of concentration, proper breathing, and, above all, maintaining a healthy body to maintain a healthy mind.

Other sports that were practiced by the Egyptian mystics included: horsemanship, running, etc. The Pharaoh, as the Perfected Man, was required to maintain perfect physical condition, and he was required to go through annual endurance exercises such as running.

5.6 MIND GAMES

People of all classes and the neteru (gods/goddesses) themselves are depicted in Ancient Egyptian tombs and temples as playing all types of games. Such games included board games as well as physical activities and sporting events.

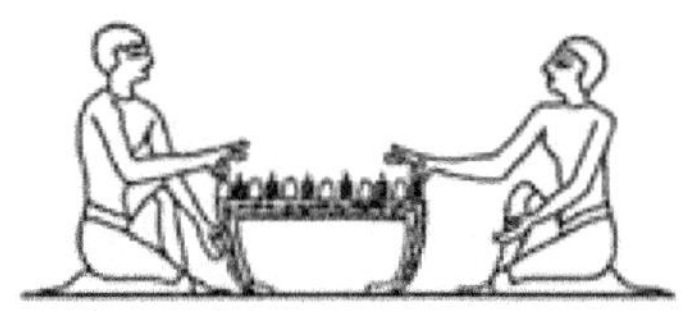

Ancient and classical writers affirmed that games owe their development, if not their very origin, to religious observances. Many accounts of games are mentioned by Homer as essential to the accompaniment of devotional ceremonies.

Games sharpen concentration, memory, patterns, etc.; and in the process, participants have fun.

5.7 CONTEMPLATION AND MEDIATION (ASTRAL TRAVEL)

According to the Sufis, the human soul 'consists of a threefold hierarchical structure: sensory, psychic, and spiritual', and 'the way of Sufism is to become aware of the possibilities that exist within the human form, to conceive them, and then, through spiritual practices, actualize them'. That process takes place through a conscious technique of contemplation and mediation to achieve communication with 'the Realities' of the universe.

In order for the Egyptian mystical seeker to learn about the world of existence that lies beyond the limitations of our human senses, he must be able to free his soul from his body. In other words, he must reach an ecstatic state of being.

Mystical seekers learn to increase their focus in order to prepare for an out-of-body experience by entering a dark, isolated place and/or blindfolding one's eyes. Some mystical seekers lie down in makeshift coffins and imagine that his/her soul hovers over his/her body. Later training allows this part of you to travel to adjoining rooms, etc.

5.8 GROUP ASTRAL TRAVEL PRACTICES

In order to gain knowledge (gnosis) through ecstatic revelations, members of the Egyptian mystic fellowships (Orders) perform a group practice commonly known as *zikr*. This practice achieves the connectedness of body, mind, and spirit which the Egyptian mystical seekers use to induce the ecstasy that leads to gaining knowledge about the world which lies beyond the limitations of our human senses.

The practice consists of using breath control, head and body movements, and chanting in a ritualistic dance, performed to tunes provided by musicians and singers.

[More about the *zikr* in next chapter and in other parts of this book.]

5.9 ENDURING LOVE (MIND OVER MATTER)

The sensation of spiritual liberation comes as a result of the triumph of mind over matter. The gradual training of the mind makes it overcome/tolerate pain. This pain threshold is progressively expanded by gradational training. Ultimately, one feels no pain. Endurance is important to achieve any goal in life, as per the common saying: "No pain, no gain."

The Egyptian mystical fellowship of *Rifaiya* is remarkable for the wonderful way in which their spiritual exaltation triumphs over pain and physical limitations. Their walking in fire and eating the white hot embers (and also glass and poisonous creatures—things which normally cause death or the most grievous bodily disturbances) have never been explained on material grounds. They usually show their talents in Egyptian mouleds; especially in the El Desouki Mouled festival.

Chapter 6 : The Way to Revelations

6.1 NO CHOSEN PEOPLE

In the Egyptian model of mysticism, revelations are accessible to anyone who aspires to seek them. There are no "special" people chosen by God to receive His revelations. In the hierarchy of existence, the human being is the image of the First Principle. By using his capacity for knowledge, the human being may ascend to the highest levels by contemplating his own reality in the mirror of God's existence.

Egyptian mysticism encompasses basically two types of spiritual experience:

1. A quest for spiritual self-development in the form of ethical self-control and worldly personal religious insight. The aspirant who is able to purify himself [as detailed earlier] is now ready for the second quest.

2. The quest to find God in the manifested world as well as finding the manifested world in God. This is accomplished through gaining knowledge by using both intellect and intuition in order to transcend the limitations of our human senses. [Developing intuitive modes of consciousness will be explained later in this chapter and in other parts of this book.]

6.2 RE—THE UNITY OF MULTIPLICITY

The ultimate goal of the Egyptian mystical seeker is to realize

Unity in multiplicity and multiplicity in the Unity of the universe. In Ancient Egyptian traditions, Re represents the primeval, cosmic, creative force. The *Litany* describes Re as *The One Joined Together, Who Comes Out of His Own Members*. The Ancient Egyptian definition of Re is:

1. The perfect representation of the Unity that comprises the putting together of the many diverse entities.

2. Re's twin term (*The One Joined Together, Who Comes Out of His Own Members*) shows the two-step metaphor of the puzzle—step one involving joining the pieces, and step two of seeing all the pieces as one unit.

Re is written as a circle with a dot or point in the center. The symbol for Ra represents both ends of the alchemical spiritual path, as follows:

– Center = cause/nothingness
– Circumference = effect/manifestation

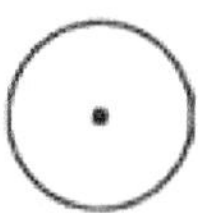

The mirror image of both ends of the Path (Ben and Neb) is used in the metaphor of the reflective mirror, in order to understand the universe and its cosmic unity. The mirror is the means of reconciling opposites and perceiving the connection between the 'phenomenal world' and the 'spiritual world' and thus understanding the 'multiplicity in unity'.

At earlier stages, man sees only pieces of things because his mind is fixed in a pattern designed to see things piecemeal, controlled by the limitation of a few senses. By healing the multiplicity within, the mystic experiences the world as whole and unified.

There is only one Essence, and all manifestations of that One Essence are, in reality, One.

6.3 DUALISM—THE ESSENCE OF CREATION

To achieve unity, we must put the pieces together. To accomplish such an objective, we need to study, know, and realize the essence of creation—namely, dualism.

The world as we know it—from the smallest particle to the largest planet—is kept in balance by a law that is based on the balanced dual nature of all things (wholes, units). Without polarized dualities, there would be no creation; i.e. no universe. Among noticeable polarized pairs are: male and female, odd and even, negative and positive, active and passive, yes and no, true and false. Each pair represents a different aspect of the same fundamental principle of polarity, and each aspect partakes of the nature of unity and of the nature of duality.

Adam/**Atam** [see chapter 3] is the Perfect Person who combines both the male and female principles. The nature of duality is best expressed in the Ancient Egyptian text known as the *Bremner-Rhind Papyrus*:

> ***I was anterior to the Two Anteriors that I made, for I had priority over the Two Anteriors that I made, for my name was anterior to theirs, for I made them anterior to the Two Anteriors...***

The dual principle in the creation state was expressed in the pair of Shu and Tefnut. The pair of husband and wife is the characteristic Egyptian way of expressing duality and polarity. This dual nature was manifested in Ancient Egyptian texts and traditions. The most ancient known texts of the Old Kingdom (ca. 4,500 years ago), namely the *Unas Funerary* (Pyramid) *Texts* §1652, express this dual nature:

This is a very powerful analogy because we use the term 'spitting image' to mean 'exactly like the original'.

The principle of dualism is also found in our perception of the universe. It seems that there are basically two aspects of the universe: the physical that we can sense, and the metaphysical that we don't see and hear—not because it does not exist, but because its frequency is outside the range of what our senses can detect. There is no distinction between a metaphysical state of being and one with a material body (as now accepted in scientific circles, since Einstein's relativity theory which states that matter is a form of energy; a coagulation or condensation of energy). As such, the universe is basically a hierarchy of energies at different orders of density. Our senses are most familiar with matter—the densest form of energy.

This matrix of energies came as a result of the initial act of creation and the subsequent effects of the Big Bang that created the universe. This matrix consists of an organized hierarchy. Each level of the hierarchy of existence is a theophany—a creation by the consciousness of the level of being above it. The self-contemplation by each stage of existence brings into being each lower stage. As such, the hierarchy of energies is interrelated, and each level is sustained by the level below it. This hierarchy of energies is set neatly into a vast matrix of deeply-interfaced natural laws. It is both physical and metaphysical.

6.4 RECONCILIATION OF DUALITIES (TYING/UNTYING THE KNOT)

In order for the mystical seeker to find the Divine Essence, one must progress in the reverse sequence of creation. In other words, the soul's progress in the journey along the Path is the upward movement from the sphere of the manifested created world, reconstructing/reassembling the pieces into one unit again, as it was prior to the Big Bang that created the world.

As stated in chapter 4, the active faculties of the Perfected Man are the heart and the tongue, and the role of everyone is to use both faculties to unite the dual aspects of the manifested world. This theme permeates Ancient Egypt, whereby both Horus and Thoth are depicted in numerous places, performing the symbolic act of uniting The Two Lands [see definition of Two Lands (which has nothing to do with areas of Egypt) in the Glossary].

To be married is to tie the knot, just like the Ancient Egyptian symbolic rite of uniting The Two Lands. Harmonizing the opposites is tying the balanced polarities in a marriage-type form. Everything in Ancient Egypt (and Sufism) is about the marriage of balanced polarities. When apparent opposites are reconciled (through intellect and intuition), the mystical seeker becomes complete, transcends the bounds of ordinary humanity, and becomes immensely powerful. When tying two polarized opposites, the mystic makes the two parts into one. In other words: to tie is to resolve apparent differences; i.e. to find that opposites are two sides of the same coin. Each pair represents a different aspect of the same fundamental principle of polarity, and each aspect partakes of the nature of unity and the nature of duality. When the mystical seeker reaches the second level of consciousness, he recognizes the dual principle in everything in the universe. One example is to find the male and female aspects in each one of us, then learn to harmonize/reconcile them.

The third and final level of consciousness is reached when the mystical seeker finds that the dual nature of a thing is the thing itself—the Two are One. The simplest illustration of this level is the example of a male/female pursuing each's beloved. One appears to be the hunter and the other is the hunted. This is an artificial polarity. In reality, there is no polarity, because the hunter is the hunted and both of them are the hunt—the perfect trinity (hunt, hunter, hunted). As the saying goes: *"I chased him until he caught me"*.

Other examples of harmonizing/reconciling apparent opposites to find out that there is no distinction between:

- Sacred and mundane—a good example is the saying "one reaps what one sows". On a mundane level, this describes the farming process. On a sacred level, it means that good deeds will translate to fruitful results. In reality, there is no difference between sacred and mundane interpretations.

- Physical and metaphysical—to see a thing (with eyesight) and to see what the same thing signifies (with intellect and intuition).

- Inner and outer realities—to discover how the human being is a miniature universe, and that all the powers that operate in the universe also operate within each one of us. The essence of the Egyptian mystical progression is based on the premise that man is the microcosm in which all attributes are united.

[See *Egyptian Divinities: The All Who Are THE ONE*, by same author.]

6.5 KNOWLEDGE BY SPIRITUAL REVELATION (ZIKR)

As discussed in Chapter 2, the Egyptian mystic utilizes both intellect and intuition to gain knowledge of the nature, attributes and works of God. Knowledge through intellect alone is not enough, because of the limitation of our senses.

Egyptian mysticism is a particular method of approach to Reality, which trains and makes use of intuitive and emotional spiritual faculties that are generally dormant and latent. This training aims at dispersing the veils that hide the self from the Real, thereby becoming transformed or absorbed into the undifferentiated Unity.

The main spiritual realization practice by the Egyptian mystical seekers (Sufis) is called zikr, and its purpose is to close the gap between the physical realm/nature and metaphysical nature. This mystical practice allows the participants the opportunity to achieve knowledge of God by way of revelations. States of visionary ecstasy are brought on by groups of purified mystical seekers participating in a unified performance/exercise of chanting religious texts, rhythmic dancing, and deep breathing. The goal is to free oneself from the body and to be lifted into the presence of the higher realms of God. In such an ecstatic state, mystical knowledge will flow into the participant mystical seeker unimpeded. As a result, the heart becomes illuminated with "Reality"—the true nature of God.

Zikr was introduced into Islamized Sufism by the Egyptian, Dhu 'l-Nun al-Misri, who said, "***zikr*** is absence from oneself [by recollecting God alone]". The absence from oneself is the ideal recollection of God. The whole of Egyptian mysticism rests on the belief that when the individual self is lost, the Universal Self is found. This ecstatic trance of absence from one's self is called "intoxication" and the ecstatics are called "spiritual drunkards". The drunkenness of the mystics describes the ecstatic frame of mind in which the spirit is intoxicated with the contemplation of God—just as the body is intoxicated with wine.

By virtue of communications with the Above, as a result of practicing *zikrs*, advanced Egyptian mystics acquire such powers as telepathy, prescience, and miraculous transportation from one place to another.

The ecstatic experience that results from practicing the zikr allows the seeker to go beyond the limitations of his senses—to have a birds-eye view of the world, where he is able to find certain knowledge, patterns, meanings, etc. After the zikr practice, the seeker comes back down to earth to utilize his newfound knowledge by using his intellect in more efficient ways to put the pieces together.

Each practice of zikr provides new illumination(s), which enables the mystical seeker to utilize his intellect/reason even further, to realize the totality of the universe. Gaining knowledge is a continuous process of using both faculties of intellect and intuition, so that they interact with and enrich one another.

It should be emphasized that in the Egyptian model of mysticism, gaining knowledge (via intellect and intuition) must be channeled into continuing service to society. Both knowledge and acts are aspects of a single progressive development along the Spiritual Path.

The second level of consciousness is reached when the mystical seeker comes to realize that the source of all deeds/actions is one source. To use the metaphor of a puzzle, the second level is reached when the mystical aspirant is able to find and reassemble all the different pieces of the cosmic puzzle. Now the picture is complete, but the lines separating the pieces are still visible in his consciousness.

6.6 UNIFICATION AND DEIFICATION

The third and final level of consciousness is reached only when the mystical seeker sees the multiplicity in the universe as one indistinguishable Unity – in other words, when the mystical seeker sees the whole picture of the cosmic puzzle as one unit, with no lines/distinctions separating the pieces. This state is reached when the mystic is able to reconcile all dualities and feels no distinction between modes, adjuncts, relations, and aspects; i.e. they have all melted together in his consciousness. As a result, the mystic himself becomes melted/annihilated/ absorbed/ immersed into the Divine Essence. Immersed in Unity, he knows not any form of phenomenal being. The successful mystical seeker has therefore achieved genuine inner unity and wholeness.

The mystical seeker at this stage has accomplished the ultimate goal of the Egyptian mystics, described as the inner marriage of self and soul. In Ancient Egyptian terms, it is the inner marriage of the Ba (soul) and the Ka (self).

Ba is usually translated as 'the soul'. It is the divine, immortal essence. When the Ba departs, the body dies. The **Ba** is usually portrayed as a stork with a human head, which is the opposite of the normal depiction of **neteru** (gods/ goddesses) as human bodies with animal heads—in other words, as divine aspects of the terrestrial.

Ka is the spiritual entity that is often translated as the *personality*. The Ka does not die with the mortal body. The Ka is portrayed as a pair of arms outstretched towards heaven, yearning to unite with the **Ba**.

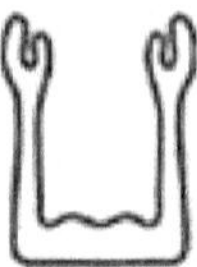

In love terms, this inner marriage of the Ba and Ka is similar to the state when the lover, beloved, and their love join to become one—the sea of love. It is the Trinity in One—The Love Triangle. This state of love unity is found in the Ancient Egyptian term MiR, which means both sea and love. The successful mystic becomes the Mir—*the Beloved Holy Sea.*

6.7 PIR: THE POWER HOUSE

When the mystic is melted into the Divine Essence, he becomes the Perfected Person or the Universal Succor, to whom all resort for aid. The ultimate constituents of all existences are drawn towards him just as iron is drawn to a magnet—and as such, he is called **qutb** (meaning 'magnetic pole'). The world of sense is subdued by his might, and he does what he wills by his power. This power house is called a Pir, an Ancient Egyptian term meaning shrine/spiritual embodiment.

The unification of the **Ba** (soul) and **Ka** (self) and their melting into the Divine **Ra** (the Creator) produces a powerful trinity known as **Ba-Ra-Ka**, a transferable quality of personal blessedness and spiritual force (almost a physical force) which allows the Pir/Mir to perform miraculous acts, demonstrate exemplary human insight, and influence and predict future events. The manifestation of this supernatural power is called **Ka-ra-ma-at/ Ka-ra-mat** (or **Ka-ramaa**), which is an Ancient Egyptian term:

Ka = the (magnetic) personality of the Pir/Mir

Ra = the Creator (his secret name is Amen)

Maat/Maa = netert (goddess) of balance/harmony

Chapter 7 : The Heavenly Helpers

The state of melting into the Divine Essence is followed (or alternates) with the state of resurrection back in the phenomenal world, in order to serve others. After having passed away from selfhood i.e. passing from plurality to unity – one must return to the phenomenal world from which he set out, and manifest unity in plurality.

In the Egyptian model, the spiritual Path consists of three journeys:

1. **Ascending**—where the aspirant travels from the world of creation to the Divine Source.

2. **Reaching and being immersed in the Divine.** At this state, the individual I-ness disappears into the Oneness of the Divine.

3. **Descending back to the world of manifestation** invested with the attributes of God, to serve—to give it all back through Ka-ra-ma-at, to his/her fellow man.

The *Pirs/Mirs* become the intermediaries between the earthly living beings and the supernatural powers in higher realms. It is the duty of *Pirs/Mirs* to use their "magical" powers to serve others both during and after their earthly existence.

They are lovingly called 'Walis'. This word is used in various senses, and is derived from its root meaning of nearness – e.g. next of kin, patron, godfather, protector, friend—whose holiness brings them near to God, and who receive from Him, as tokens of His peculiar favor, miraculous gifts (**Kara-ma-at**).

After his death, a **Wali** often becomes the patron and protector of the locality or social group in which he lived. Academic Egyptologists describe these Walis as *local* or *minor gods*.

Unlike the saints among Christians and Islamic Shiites, who are chosen by their religious authorities, Pirs/Mirs/ Walis are chosen by the ordinary Egyptian people based on their performances and their abilities to influence supernatural forces in order to assist those on Earth.

7.2 STAYING ALIVE

The Egyptians (as well as Sufi traditions) recognize that the Walis possess unearthly powers that are of the greatest service to mankind. But these powers, if not entirely dependent upon, are greatly reinforced by the presentation of food and drink offerings as well as the recitation of incantations and by performing regular ritual acts such as sacrifices, libations, communions, dances, and symbolic struggles. These are presently performed by the Egyptian mystics (Sufis) at the various shrines of the Walis on a regular basis. Inscriptions in various Egyptian temples and tomb-chapels, as well as in a number of letters, testify to the importance of such rituals. One of these letters, for example, speaks of:

> *my daughter who makes offerings to the spirit in return for watching over the earthly survivors.*

**Auset (Isis) giving bread and water
to the ba (in the form of a bird).**

Diodorus, in *Book I*, 16, affirms the role of Thoth as it relates to the significance of offerings and the ordinances required to maintain them:

> *It was by Thoth, according to the Egyptians, that . . ., and that ordinances regarding the honors and offerings due to the gods were duly established. . .*

Accordingly, Ancient and Baladi Egyptians presented/present their deceased with numerous articles of food and drink at the shrines of the Pirs/Mirs/Walis.

7.3 THE BLESSED SHRINES (THE KA HOUSES)

After the earthly death, a Pir/Mir/Wali's Ba-ra-ka (spiritual force/blessing) is thought to increase and to inhere in the persons and particularly the places associated with and chosen by him. The Pir/Mir/Wali chooses and conveys the places for his shrines to his family and friends during dreams (possibly awake, also). As a result, a shrine (or more—usually more than two) is set apart for him/her. Such shrines, in most cases, are not their tombs. The shrines are always selected by the Pirs/Mirs/Walis near specific trees, which become a type of sacred grove/garden. The descendants of the Wali frequently serve as custodians of the shrines to make them available to the visiting public, free of charge. These custodians are called

Servants of the Ka.

As stated earlier, the Ka is the essence of the person. Everyone leaves a part of himself (Ka) in everything he comes into contact with. Therefore, each shrine contains a relic(s) from the ***Pir/Mir/ Wali*** that he chose himself.

The ***Wali's*** shrine is usually a small, square, whitewashed building crowned with a dome-shaped roof that represents the shape of the sky and the Ancient Egyptian symbol for Neb (meaning gold).

The dome sits directly over a mostly-empty vault; an oblong monument of stone or brick or wood or copper usually covered with silk or linen and surrounded by a railing or screen of wood or bronze, called maksoorah.

When the ***Pir/Mir/Wali*** dies, his Ba (represented by the bird) separates from his ***Ka*** (his image/personage). To keep the Ba and the Ka of the ***Wali*** close to each other, people must visit the shrines and provide offerings on specified weekdays and annual occasions. Egyptians speak of their deceased as living, which shows how definite a belief it is that the souls of the deceased return to their shrines on the specified days of their weekly and annual visitations.

While the shrine houses the Wali's Ka (a relic of his choice), his spirit—Ba (shown as a bird)—is nearby. The depicted Ancient Egyptian illustration of the tomb/shrine of Hau shows the dome-roofed shrine with a sacred tree next to it. Note the bird depicted on the top of the tree. Over the bird is written 'Soul of Ausar'. Everyone, after leaving the earthly realm, is equated to Ausar (Osiris), and as such, the Ba represents the soul of any deceased person.

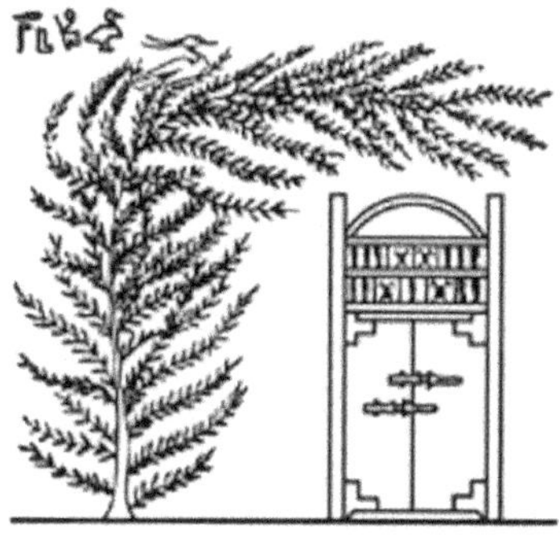

This Ancient Egyptian papyrus depicts the very same traditions continued by present-day Egyptians—a domed shrine (or shrines) next to a tree—the Tree of Life.

The combined symbolism of a domed shrine and the tree is perfectly depicted in Dendera and refers to the Isis Osiris allegory, where the coffin containing the body of Osiris was taken by the waves to the shoreline of a foreign land. A tree sprang up and grew around it, enclosing the body of Osiris in the trunk. The tree grew large, beautiful, and fragrant.

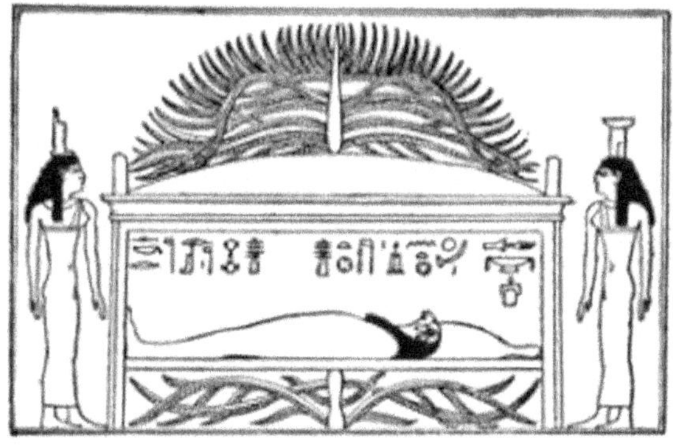

A very common practice among Ancient and Baladi Egyptians is to visit shrines. People came/come to **Walis'** shrines to ask for blessing, healing, and the goods of this life, such as marriage, children, and prosperity. Most Egyptians not only expect a blessing to follow their visiting the shrine of a folk saint, but they also dread that some misfortune will befall them if they neglect this act. At the shrines, they touch or kiss the holy place, make small gifts or sacrifices, celebrate seasonal festivals, and mark the rejuvenation day(s) of the folk saint, commonly known as **mouled/ moulid/mawlid**. The term mouled is literally translated as 'birthday'—implying a date of renewal/rejuvenation – and has nothing to do with anyone's biological birthday. Many of the **Walis** have several **mouleds** a year.

On these special occasions (**mouleds**), the **Pir/Mir/Wali** becomes an active participant. The ("deceased") **Pir/Mir/ Wali** plays an important role in the religious and cosmological framework/ operation. The hierarchy of the Walis (folk saints) upholds the order of the universe.

PART III : THE PUBLIC VISITATION FAIRS

Chapter 8 : The Cyclical Renewal Festivals

8.1 THE NEED FOR RENEWAL

The Egyptians continued their ancestors' traditions of venerating their folk saints (***Pirs/Mirs/Walis***) and visiting the shrines during their annual festivals. The aim of Egyptian festivals was (and continues to be) the rejuvenation and renewal of cosmic energies.

The main theme of the Ancient Egyptian texts is the cyclical nature of the universe and the constant need for the renewal of such cycles through well-designated festivals.

The Egyptians viewed/view these festivals as part of human existence, which constitutes the rhythm of the life of community and individual alike. This rhythm results from the order of cosmic life.

The renewal and rejuvenation of the life of the cosmos, of the community, and of the individual are affected by rites. These rites had/have the power to bring about the rejuvenation and rebirth of divine life. As such, the Ancient (and present-day) Egyptian festivals came to have the function of enactments of cosmological (religious) renewals.

Starting from the point of view that religious festivals mark the holy events in the course of life, it is easy to distinguish the following types:

1. Agrarian festivals, which are connected with agricultural work such as sowing and harvesting.

2. Seasonal festivals, which are celebrated e.g. in spring, mid-summer, and autumn.

3. Calendar-festivals, the dates of which depend on the position of the sun, the phases of the moon and the advent of the new year.

4. Family-festivals, which impart a certain cachet to important events in the life of the family.

5. Festivals of the deceased, during which the memory of the deceased is honored at regular intervals.

6. Festivals connected with events in the life of the community, which are of exceptional religious importance.

During numerous Ancient Egyptian religious festivals, the participants fall back on the archetypal truth of their cosmic consciousness (*As above so below, and as below so above*). Every holy festival actualizes the archetypal holy cycle. These holy cycles have become part of the calendar. More accurately, the calendar served to indicate when the cosmological powers (neteru/gods) and their renewal cycles were manifested. All early Greek and Roman writers affirmed this Ancient Egyptian tradition; such as Plutarch, in his *Moralia Vol. V* (377, 65):

> *. . . They [the Egyptians] associate theological concepts with the seasonal changes in the surrounding atmosphere, or with the growth of the crops and seed-times and plowing. . .*

The present-day name for the annual renewal festival is *mouled/ moulid/mawlid*, literally meaning *(renewed) birthday*. Baladi Egyptians continue to consider the festivals and their rituals as the climax of their religious practices, which are very critical to the order and harmony of the cosmos and, by extension, the well-being of one and all.

All present-day mouleds (except for Mohammed's and those of his immediate family) are a continuation of Ancient Egyptian festivals, camouflaged under Islamic names.

8.2 THE HISTORY OF MOULEDS IN EGYPT

The annual cyclical festivals (mouleds) have been a part of Ancient Egypt's traditions throughout its history. The text on the Palermo Stone (ca. 5,000 years ago) gives a list of the principal Ancient Egyptian annual festivals during the next 700 years. Among the listed festivals are the Spring Festival of Easter, Min, and the Heb-Sed Festival of the Pharaoh. The Unas Funerary (Pyramid) Texts of the 5th Dynasty record festive ceremonies that were performed on the 1st, the 6th, and the 15th of every Ancient Egyptian month.

A list of the Ancient Egyptian annual festivals was attempted by the Egyptologist Schott. It is clear from this list that regular rejuvenation festivals were very common. The temple of Medinat Habu, in Western Luxor (Thebes), lists celebrations that were held on 162 days in a year, taking place during several successive days of each month. Some of these celebrations were even repeated every day in honor of different deities during some months. The texts from the temples at Dendera, Edfu, Philae and Esna show many festivals. These lists of festivals in various temple locations are not by any means exhaustive, as they only refer to festivals that had certain significance in these temples. In addition to temple festivals, there were also numerous cyclical festivals at the noble/Pir/Mir/Wali shrines. A text from the 6th Dynasty (ca. 2300 BCE) reads as follows:

> *A coming-forth-unto-the-voice* (meaning the rise/wake) *for him in his tomb-chapel at the monthly and half-monthly festi-*

A classic example of the rules and regulations of the festivals related to the folk saints/Walis' veneration are the ten texts found in Asyut, which are attributed to Hepzefi during the time of Sesostris I (c. 2000 BCE). The texts detail activities that are exactly the same as in present-day mouleds in Egypt.

The Islamized academia claim that the mouleds began in Egypt in the 10th century CE. Historical records prove that they began thousands of years earlier. The Islamic rule (post 641 CE) of Egypt forced people to give Islamic names to ancient traditions.

The similarities between ancient and present traditions indicate that the modern ceremonies (called mouleds) are pre-Christian and pre-Islamic in origin, and are direct ritualistic survivals from the earliest period of Egyptian history.

The official annual number of mouleds in present-day Egypt, even though it is contrary to Islam, is estimated at more than 3,000. There is not a single day in Egypt without a mouled somewhere, and the participation is very profound. For example, just the three main festivals of the Sidi Ahmed el-Badawi, at the city of Tanta, attract almost as many visitors as Mecca does pilgrims from the whole of the Islamized world. The major Autumn mouled of el-Badawi is attended by more than two million people, and each of the other two mouleds are attended by more than one million visitors. All this is indicative of the Baladi Egyptian mystics' adherence, by the millions, to their ancient traditions.

8.3 THE FESTIVAL REGULATORS (ISIS AND OSIRIS)

The concept of Isis and Osiris was the Egyptian model used to explain all facets of knowledge, as was noted by all early Greek and Roman historians. That concept was also utilized for setting the dates, natures, and objectives of each festival.

The most significant (but not the only) aspect of Isis and Osiris is best described by Diodorus of Sicily, *Book I* (11, 5-6), as follows:

These two neteru (gods), they hold, regulate the entire universe, giving both nourishment and increase to all things by means of a system of three seasons which complete the full cycle through an unobservable movement. . .

This concept was affirmed by Plutarch in his *Moralia Vol. V* (377, 65), as follows:

They [the Egyptians] associate theological concepts with the seasonal changes in the surrounding atmosphere, or with the growth of the crops and seed-times and plowing; as examples the Egyptians say that Osiris is being buried at the time when the grain is sown and covered in the earth and that he comes to life and reappears when plants begin to sprout. For this reason also it is said that Isis, when she perceived that she was pregnant, put upon herself an amulet on the sixth day of the month Phaophi; and about the time of the winter solstice she gave birth to Harpocrates, imperfect and premature, amid the early flowers and shoots. For this reason they bring to him as an offering the first-fruits of growing lentils, and the days of his birth they celebrate after the spring equinox.

8.4 SETTING THE DATES (REJUVENATION CYCLES)

From the records of early historians, such as Plutarch, Herodotus and Diodorus, as well as the hundreds of festival records throughout Ancient Egypt, it is clear that setting the dates of these festivals was synchronized with cosmological rhythms. Setting the dates of both ancient and present-day festivals were/ are subject to three cycles, individually or a combination of two or all three. The three cycles are:

1. The solar cycle that commands the seasons with all that that implies. The Egyptians developed and followed the Sothic calendar, which is associated with Isis, representing the solar principle in the universe. [See *Egyptian Cosmology: The Animated Universe*, by same author, for details.]

Since the Islamic occupation of Egypt (641 CE), this calendar is known as the "Coptic" calendar, even though it was developed thousands of years before Christianity.

2. The lunar cycle that governs fertility and other biological periodicities, as well as various meteorological phenomena.

Many of the Ancient Egyptian and present-day mouleds were/ are celebrated at (or in conjunction with) the new or the full moon. The lunar principle in the universe is represented by Osiris, who was called *Osiris the Moon*.

3. The day of the week, which is related to the seven planets and the seven musical notes.

The relationship between the seven days of the week and the seven harmonic natural sounds of the diatonic scale was instituted by the Ancient Egyptians. Such a relationship was a consequence of the heavenly music of the seven (wandering) planets. Dio Cassius (2nd century CE) in his volumes *Roman History* (Book XXXVII, Section 18), stated:

> *The custom of referring the days to the seven stars called planets was instituted by the Egyptians. . .*
> *. . .and to them already an ancestral tradition. . .*

As a consequence of utilizing a combination of the three cycles, many festival dates may vary widely from year to year, just like the Easter celebration, which is also determined according to three Egyptian elements: a weekday that follows a full moon, which follows the vernal equinox (i.e. a solar cycle). We therefore must recognize that festival dates in Ancient Egyptian buildings indicate dates at a specific year(s). Consequently, we occasionally find different dates for the same festival in different years, just as we similarly have a different date for Easter every year.

The annual calendar of the Egyptian cyclical festivals (mouleds) determine each date's, function(s) and the venerated deities/ Walis related to each occasion. The intent is to synchronize our mode of communication (as below) with various cyclical patterns in the universe (so above).

Some significant points about the Egyptian cyclical calendar of events (past or present) include:

- The calendar is compiled by a few specialists who know the significant pattern and cycle of each festival. Just like in our present times, only a few people know how to set the date for Easter. In Egypt, it is/was likewise. This is confirmed in *Herodotus, Book Two* (58-59):

  > *"It was the Egyptians too who originated, and taught the Greeks to use ceremonial meetings, processions, and processional offerings: a fact which can be inferred from the obvious antiquity of such ceremonies in Egypt, compared with Greece, where they have been only recently introduced. The Egyptians meet in assembly not once a year only, but on a number of occasions. There is a sacred tradition which accounts both for the date and for the manner of these observances. . ."*

- There are several related festivals (mouleds) that are observed in certain cyclical sequences, and as such are separated by a set period. Some festivals are spaced at specific cycles—such as 7, 40 or 50 days from other more prominent events. Each of these cycles has its own significance. A comparable example in the Christian ecclesiastical calendar is Easter, which is tied to Lent, Ascension Day, and Pentecost.

- The most common example in Egypt of the weekly cycle is the relationship of many festivals to those of Sidi el-Badawi of

Tanta. Many festivals follow Badawi's three annual festivals exactly a week later.

- The 40-day cycle signifies the time to die or to be reborn. The Egyptians believe that it takes 40 days to die (prior to actual death) and 40 days (after actual death) for the soul to leave the body completely. Consequently, the mummification (body dehydration) period lasted 40 days.

- 50 days is associated with renewal. This was illustrated in the Ancient Egyptian model story when Seth, after disposing of Osiris, ruled as a tyrant for 50 "days" before Seth was replaced by Horus—representing the resurrection/renewal of Osiris.

- There were/are several nativities for the same occasion, to correspond to several related cycles in the year that are/were associated with such an occasion. Such a point was noted by Plutarch, in *Moralia Vol. V* (372, 52B):

  ". . .as is written in the records entitled the Birthdays (plural) *of Horus."*

This tradition continues in our present times where, for example, Sidi el-Badawi of Tanta has three major festivals annually. Most other Walis have two or more festivals at one or several shrines.

- Every location/region had/has certain holy days peculiarly consecrated to their patrons, in addition to those common to the regions beyond each locality.

- Festivals usually last one week and a day. Most mouleds vary in their beginning weekday, but many begin on a Friday and end on the afternoon of the next Friday. The typical eight day duration is consistent with Ancient Egyptian traditions. Musically, the renewal theme of eight terms corresponds to the octave because it reaches through all eight intervals of the scale (the eight white keys of the keyboard).

Eight is the number of Thoth, and at Khmunu (Hermopolis), Thoth is called the *Master of the City of Eight*.

Every day has its peculiar activities and each tetra-chord (4 days) has its own energy theme.

The eve of the last day of the octave-week festival is called the Great Night/Evening—it is the climax of the festival [as will be detailed later on].

- It is important to remember that all Egyptian mouleds (except for those assigned to Mohammed and his family) follow the Ancient Egyptian solar calendar, and not the Islamic purely lunar reckoning.
- The Islamic names of the Egyptian mouleds are a sheer facade to protect and maintain ancient traditions.
- Sunset marks the beginning of the day in Ancient and Baladi (Sufi) traditions. As such, an apparent discrepancy of one day between Egyptian dates and the adopted Western reckoning is possible in some festival dates that are shown in this book.

Chapter 9 : Samples of Ancient-Present Festivals

9.1 FAMILIAR FESTIVALS

The following is a sample of familiar Ancient/present Egyptian festivals, showing their dates, nature, and traditions.

The sample festivals show/confirm:

1. The cyclical patterns stated in the previous chapter.
2. The Egyptian connectivity between the cyclical cosmological patterns and earthly activities.
3. The conceptual role of Osiris and Isis in the Egyptian festivals as shown in the previous chapter.
4. That Ancient Egyptian festivals are continued in present-day mouleds.
5. That the Christian annual festivals are an adoption of Ancient Egyptian festivals.

The dates provided in the sample festivals are based on the Ancient Egyptian calendar (which is still in use under the name *Coptic* Calendar), as well as the equivalent date in the Latin calendar.

9.2 THE EGYPTIAN CALENDRICAL NEW YEAR'S DAY

The Egyptian calendrical New Year's Day currently corresponds to 11 September of the Latin calendar.

Not coincidentally, the ecclesiastical year that is followed by the

Orthodox churches, according to Byzantine practices like Ancient Egypt, also begins on the 11th of September.

9.3 THE WAG FESTIVAL

The last day of the Ancient Egyptian Wag Festival was celebrated, according to Plutarch [*Moralia Vol. V* (378,68)], on the 19th of Toot (27 September). It was common for those who attended to greet each other with expressions like ***"How sweet a thing is truth!"*** or ***"The tongue is fortune, the tongue is god!"***.

This festival signifies that the River Nile has risen to its greatest height, or nearly so. Osiris represents the rising water. Osiris is also known as the ***Manifester of Truth***—hence, the Egyptians said, ***"How sweet a thing is truth!"*** The second phrase relates to Thoth, whose symbol was/is the *tongue*. Hence, the Egyptians said: ***"The tongue is fortune, the tongue is god!"***

The same festival/mouled continues to be celebrated, to date, camouflaged in a Christian/Islamic pretense. Some call it *the Cross*, or *Mar Barsoum el Eleryan* Festival, or *Mohammed Barsoom* Festival/Mouled.

=> __100 days later is the Eve of 6 January—the Epiphany/ Rebirth of Osiris as the renewed Horus.__

9.4 THE CONCEPTION (PLANTING) MOULED

In the typical Egyptian story form, forty days after Isis' birthday [see last page in this chapter] – i.e. on 6 Babeh/ Phaophi (17 October) – Isis was impregnated by Osiris. Accordingly, Ancient (and present-day) Egyptians planted seeds throughout Egypt on this date in a special mouled with special rituals to ensure a successful harvest.

Planting is the *burying* of seed into earth. As such, planting is associated with *burial—death* that leads to a resurrection (i.e. sprouting). This beautiful analogy was described by Plutarch in his *Moralia, Vol. V* (377, 65), where we read:

> "*. . . the Egyptians say that <u>Osiris is being buried at the time when the grain is sown</u> and covered in the earth and that he comes to life and reappears when plants begin to sprout. For this reason also it is said that Isis, when she perceived that she was pregnant, put upon herself an amulet on the sixth day of the month Phaophi*" [equivalent to 17 October in the Latin calendar]. . .

Osiris represents the process, growth, and underlying cyclical aspects of the universe—the principle that makes life come from apparent death. The most impressive representation of the concept of regeneration, namely Osiris, is the illustration depicting Osiris with 28 stalks of wheat growing out of his coffin. [See an illustration later in this chapter.]

On this very prominent day, present-day Egyptians commemorate one of three major annual mouleds of Sidi el Badawi in Tanta, where the official attendance is more than two million people.

=> <u>**40 days after planting the seeds, the Egyptians celebrated/ celebrate the event of the Last Supper and the Loss of Osiris.**</u>

9.5 THE LAST SUPPER (DARKNESS OVERTAKES LIGHT)

Forty days after the burial of Osiris' seeds into Mother Earth,

Isis/Osiris met his demise. In the typical Ancient Egyptian story form, Plutarch writes in his *Moralia, Vol. V* (356, 13) about how Osiris was invited by Seth to a feast where Seth and his accomplices tricked Osiris into laying down in a makeshift coffin. Plutarch continues with:

> *"...and those who were in the plot ran to it and slammed down the lid, which they fastened by nails from the outside and also by using molten lead. Then they carried the chest to the river and sent it on its way to the sea through the Tanitic Mouth. Wherefore the Egyptians even to this day name this mouth the hateful and execrable. Such is the tradition. They say also that the date on which this deed was done was the 17th day of Athor* [27 November], *when the sun passes through Scorpion."*

The events of 17 Hatoor/Athor (27 November), as reported by Plutarch, have all the elements of the biblical Jesus' Last Supper; i.e. a conspiracy, feast, friends, and betrayal. However, for the Ancient Egyptians, there are other meanings to the story. Plutarch, in *Moralia, Vol. V* (366, 39D), wrote:

> *"The story told of the shutting up of Osiris in the chest seems to <u>mean nothing else than the vanishing and disappearance of water</u>. . . at the time when. . . the Nile recedes to its low level and the land becomes denuded. As the nights grow longer, the <u>darkness increases, and the potency of the light is abated and subdued</u>. . ."*

The *antagonistic* relationship between Osiris and Seth—as it relates to environmental conditions—is mentioned by Plutarch, *Moralia, Vol. V* (364, 33B), as such:

> *"... The Egyptians <u>simply give the name of Osiris to the whole source and faculty creative of moisture</u>, believing this to be the cause of generation and the substance of life-producing seed; and the name of <u>Seth they give to all that is dry, fiery, and arid</u>,*

The Loss of Osiris is now celebrated in the Abu Sefein Mouled at the same time and with the same traditions; i.e. a big feast followed by a 40-day cycle of figurative death by fasting and other disciplinary means.

=> **28 days after the Last Supper is the birth/rebirth of the renewed king on 25 December.**

=> **40 days after the Last Supper is Epiphany.**

9.6 THE ADVENT OF OSIRIS

Osiris' life, being a symbol of the moon, is associated with a cycle of 28 days (4 weeks). This was echoed later in the Christian Advent, which, in 'Latin', is *ad-venio*, meaning *to come to*. The Catholic Encyclopedia admits that: "***Advent is a period embracing 4 Sundays. The first Sunday may be as early as 27 November, and then Advent has 28 days.***" As noted above, 27 November is the date of the symbolic Last Supper, Death, and Loss of Osiris.

The 28-day cycle of Osiris and its relationship to the regeneration principle is nicely depicted in the famed scene of the resurrection of the wheat, which depicts Osiris with 28 stalks of wheat growing out of his coffin.

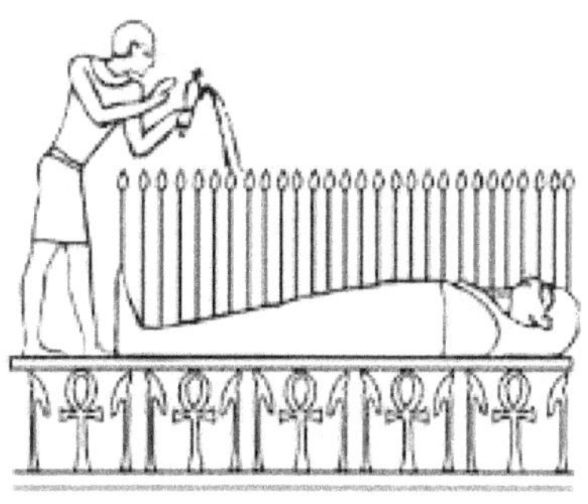

The ecclesiastical year begins with Advent in the Western churches. According to the Catholic Encyclopedia, "the faithful are admonished, during this time:

- To prepare themselves worthy to celebrate the anniversary of the Lord *coming into the world as the incarnate God of love,*

- Thus to make their souls fitting abodes for the Redeemer coming in Holy Communion and through grace, and

- Thereby to make themselves ready for *His final coming as judge, at death and at the end of the world."*

All the above elements are of Ancient Egyptian origin. Such traditions were observed during (and in fact were based on) the annual jubilee of the Ancient Egyptian King, known as the Sed (or Heb-Sed) Festival, which was always held during the month of Kee-hek (Khoiakh, i.e. December) every year. This festival dates from time immemorial, and continued to be celebrated throughout Ancient Egyptian history.

The intent of this annual event was the renewal/rejuvenation of the supernatural powers of the [reigning] King. The renewal rituals aimed at bringing a new life force to the King; i.e. a (figurative) death and a (figurative) rebirth of the reigning King.

In Ancient Egyptian traditions, the rejuvenation/birthday of a new/renewed King symbolically comes 28 days after 27 November, the symbolic Last Supper and the *Death* of Osiris; i.e. 25 December. The Christian calendar celebrates the same day as the birth (rebirth) of the new King, namely Jesus, who is referred to as a King throughout the Bible. The 28-day cycle signifies the Advent (both in Ancient Egyptian and Christian traditions) of the King. [For more information about Jesus as a King, see *Ancient Egyptian Roots of Christianity* by Moustafa Gadalla.]

All the elements mentioned in the Catholic Encyclopedia mentioned above concur with their Egyptian origins, whereby Osiris *incarnates* as Horus and Osiris became *the judge of the dead.*

Due to the absolute lack of historical and archaeological evidence to support the biblical accounts of Jesus' birth, life, and death, and in order for the Christian church to set a birth date of some kind, they turned to Egypt. Practically all churches picked their dates from an Ancient Egyptian list which was attributed to Clement of Alexandria. The list places several dates: 25 Pachon (20 May), 24 or 25 Pharmuthi (19 or 20 April). Clement, however, indicated that Epiphany (and with it, probably the Nativity) was celebrated on 15 or 11 of Tobi (10 or 6 January). 6 January is proven to be the date adopted for his "birthday" throughout the various churches in the Mediterranean Basin. 25 December came later. and was based on the Julian calendar, which is 13 days behind 6 January.

9.7 THE KING'S NEW YEAR'S DAY (JANUARY 1)

As noted earlier, typical Egyptian festivals extend for an octave-week. As such, the Egyptian King's renewal day of 25 December (Julian calendar) has its climax in its octave (8 days later) on 1 January—the New Year's Day for the rejuvenated King. On the 22nd of Kee-hek/ Khoiakh (1 January), during the annual jubilee festivities, a special ceremony was held, at which a ceremonial voyage was led by the effigy of Osiris, accompanied by 34 images of divinities in 34 little boats illuminated by 365 candles—the candles representing the number of days in a regular year.

9.8 EPIPHANY (JANUARY 6)

A cycle of forty days after the Egyptian Last Supper (27 November) and the death of Osiris was/is the Epiphany on 6 January which was later adopted in the Christian calendar of events for the same objective.

Like the Ancient Egyptian traditions, the original intent of

Epiphany in the Eastern Church is for one about to be baptized—the sacrament of Baptism. As stated earlier, baptism represents figurative death and rebirth. A bornagain cycle typically takes 40 days (from 27 November to 6 January). At the end of the cycle, people bathe in the Nile (baptism), and the fast is broken. Happy days are here again.

9.9 LENT

Lent denotes the 40 days' fast that precedes the Holy Week of Easter. One has to (figuratively) die in order to be (figuratively) reborn. Lent represents the figurative death (fasting, self-discipline, etc.) before rebirth.

Lent and Easter pre-date Christianity, as explained below. Lent was, in origin, the time of the final preparation for candidates for the solemn rite of baptism at the Easter Vigil. The ritual of baptism was performed in the sacred lakes of the Ancient Egyptian temples and in the River Nile itself.

9.10 EASTER

It has been common knowledge that the Christian Easter was not an historical event, but that the festival pre-dated Christianity. Webster's Dictionary describes Easter as the "name of pagan vernal festival almost coincident in date with paschal festival of the church". The so-called "pagan" festival is the Egyptian Easter. In the Egyptian (and later, the Christian) calendar, Easter is the center of the greater part of the ecclesiastical year from Septuagesima to the last Sunday after Pentecost, the feast of the Ascension, Pentecost, Corpus Christi, and all other movable feasts, because they are tied to the Easter date.

Commemorating Easter is the cornerstone upon which the Christian faith is built. Yet, the Apostolic Fathers do not mention it because it was a continuation of an existing Jewish holiday—namely Passover—which in turn was/is an adoption of an Ancient Egyptian Spring festival.

Ancient Egyptian records indicate that the Egyptian Spring Festival was in existence at least since the Old Kingdom. The purpose of such a festival was/is the renewal of nature in the springtime, when life returns once more to the world.

As stated earlier, Osiris represents the cyclical nature of the universe; the principle that makes life come from apparent death. It was, therefore, natural that Osiris be identified with Spring, on the day when he was believed to have risen from the dead.

The Easter celebration, like all Egyptian festivals, lasts an octave-week (known in the Christian calendar as the Holy Week, extending from Palm Sunday to Easter Sunday). The Ancient Egyptian Holy Week is followed by Easter Monday—known in Egypt as *Sham en Neseem*. This is the only official national holiday that has survived since Ancient Egyptian times.

As an extension of the Ancient Egyptian traditions, numerous mouleds are held throughout Egypt during the Easter Holy Week by the Egyptian mystics (Sufis). One of these events is the annual (non-Christian) Mouled of Abu-Hareera, which is held in Giza.

9.11 ASCENSION DAY

In the Ancient Egyptian tradition, the spirit of the deceased takes 40 days to completely depart the body and ascend to the heavens. Accordingly, the mummification (body dehydration) period lasted 40 days. Likewise, the Christian calendar commemorates Ascension Day on the 40th day after Easter, when it celebrates "the bodily ascent of Jesus into Heaven, on the 40th day after resurrection".

9.12 THE FIRST TEARDROP

After Osiris ascended to the heavens, his wife Isis began weeping. The Eve of the 11th of the Ancient Egyptian month of Ba-oo-neh (18 June) is called "Leylet en-Nuktah" (or the Night of the Tear Drop), as it commemorates the first drop that falls into the Nile to begin the annual flood season. Astrologers calculate the precise moment when the "drop" is to fall, which is always in the course of the night above mentioned. This Ancient Egyptian celebration is recognized in northern Cairo as *Mouled el Embabi*.

This ancient festival was particularly welcomed by the Egyptian peasants all along the Nile Valley. Diodorus of Sicily tells us how the husbandmen indulged in recreations of every kind, and showed their gratitude to God for the benefits of the inundation. According to Heliodorus, it was one of the principal festivals of the Egyptians. Libanius asserts that these rites were deemed of so much importance by the Egyptians throughout the land that unless they were performed at the proper season, and in a becoming manner, by the persons appointed to this duty, they believed that the Nile would refuse to rise and inundate the land.

The Nile begins to rise about, or soon after, the period of the summer solstice. Two weeks after the first teardrop (i.c. from, or about, the 27th of the month Ba-oo-neh [3rd of July]), the incremental increases in the water level of the Nile were proclaimed daily in the streets of the city, as stated by Plutarch, and were continued by Baladi Egyptians until the Aswan High Dam was built in the 1960s.

One of the most compelling parts of the Egyptian Model Story of Isis and Osiris is how these two symbols relate to the flood season in Egypt. The Egyptians associated the beginning of the flood with Isis after her husband/soulmate (namely, Osiris), ascended to heaven 40 days after his death, when she started weeping, begging her dead husband to rise again. Egyptians associated the first teardrop with the beginning of the rise of the Nile. Isis continued to weep, wishing for her husband to rise.

The beauty here is that Isis wishes her husband to rise from the dead, and the water of the Nile is consequently rising, as well. It should be noted that the water of the Nile is symbolized by Osiris himself.

Plutarch described this relationship in his *Moralia, Vol. V* (366, 38A), as follows:

> *". . As the Egyptians regard the Nile as the effusion of Osiris, so they hold and believe the earth to be the body of Isis, not all of it, but so much of it as the Nile covers, fertilizing it and uniting with it. From this union they make Horus to be born. . .'*

In other words, Isis recreates/regenerates Osiris from her tears every year. Her tears are blood-red in color, which is the same color of the floodwaters, since this water comes as a result of the rainy season in Ethiopia, which erodes the silt of the Ethiopian highlands and carries it towards Egypt along the Blue Nile and other tributaries. So, Isis' tears represent this reddish color of the water during the flood season. In essence, Isis is *crying a river*—so to speak. The Christian faithful follow the same Ancient Egyptian traditions in their presentations of the statues of Mary with bloody teardrops coming out of her eyes.

=> **It should be noted that from 3 July (the actual beginning of the rise of the Nile) to Assumption Day (22 August) is 50 days—a Pentecost.**

9.13 THE EGYPTIAN PENTECOST

The Apostles' (Prophets) Mouled in Egypt is held 50 days after Easter. Likewise, in the Christian calendar, the faithful celebrate Pentecost, which happens 50 days after Easter. Pentecost celebrates "the descent of the Holy Spirit upon the Apostles".

This festival is of Ancient Egyptian origin. Pentecost signifies the period of the Khamaseen (meaning, The Fifty), when the annual hot and reddish sandstorms and winds are of frequent occurrence. This annual event commences on the day immediately following Good Friday, i.e. Easter (Light) Saturday, and ceases on the Day of Pentecost (or Whitesunday)—an interval of 50 days.

This Pentecostal event is related to the Ancient Egyptian allegory about Isis and Osiris: after Osiris was killed, Seth became the king of Egypt, and he ruled oppressively. Seth represents the color red and the oppressive weather that is dry, fiery, and arid. In essence, Seth represents the red, hot cloud of dust, Khamaseen.

At the time of his death, Osiris and Isis had no children; but by mystical and "magical" means, Osiris impregnated Isis. As a result, Isis conceived a son, Horus, who was raised secretly in the marshes of the Nile Delta. The allegory continues that as soon as Horus had grown to manhood, he challenged Seth for the right to the throne. After several battles between them, they went to the council of the twelve neteru (gods, goddesses) to determine who should rule. The council decided that Osiris/ Horus should regain the throne of Egypt, and Seth should rule over the deserts/wastelands. In weather terms, this decision by the council ended the 50 days of oppressive weather (the Khamaseen). The date of judgment by the council of neteru/apostles/prophets was declared to be Whitesunday (White-Sunday), meaning: the 50 reddish days are over (i.e.: it's all clear now).

9.14 TRANSFIGURATION OF HORUS

Fifty days after Isis' first teardrop (on 17 June), on 6 August, the Ancient Egyptians celebrated the reappearance of Osiris in the form of the resurrected Horus. This was confirmed by Plutarch in his *Moralia, Vol. V* (372,52B):

> *"In the sacred hymns of Osiris they call upon him who is hidden in the arms of the Sun; and on the thirtieth of the month Epiphi* [6 August]*they celebrate the birthday of the Eyes of Horus, at the time when the Moon and the Sun are in a perfectly straight line, since they regard not only the Moon but also the Sun as the eye and light of Horus."*

This is identical with the later Christians' claim of the transfiguration of Jesus, celebrated by the Orthodox Church on 6 August. This holiday commemorates the "revelation of Jesus' divinity to Peter, James, and John".

This Ancient Egyptian tradition continues, camouflaged in the Mouled of El-Desouki, at the town of Desouk on the east bank of the westerly branch of the Nile River. El Desouki is lovingly known as Abu-el-e-nane (of the two eyes), just like *Horus, the Elder of the Two Eyes.*

The two eyes of Horus mentioned by Plutarch are the sun and the moon, symbols of his parents, Isis and Osiris. As stated earlier, Isis represents the solar principle in the universe, and Osiris represents the lunar principle in the universe.

This mouled is recognized by the best magical (divination) acts in Egypt, which correspond to the later Christian celebration whose main theme is the "revelation of (Jesus) divinity".

9.15 OUR LADY MERIAM (ASSUMPTION OF OUR LADY DAY)

In typical Egyptian story form, Isis finished her crying over her soul mate Osiris in about the middle of August, which means that Isis cried all the tears she had. It is at this point in time that the Egyptians (both ancient and modern) hold a festival signifying the last teardrop from Isis which will cause the peak of the flood level. It is during this celebration that the Egyptians throw an effigy of Isis into the waters, to symbolize that Isis drowned in her own tears. Incredibly, the church has adopted the same exact date to represent the ascension of the "Virgin Mary" to heaven as Assumption Day, which is defined as:

> *The dogma of the taking up of the body and soul of the Virgin Mary (**Auset** is also a virgin) into heavens after her death.*

The Orthodox Church celebrates Assumption Day on 15 August,

which is the same exact day when present-day Egyptians observe the end of the rainy season in Ethiopia.

In addition to official governmental celebrations, the Baladi Egyptians hold a mouled called *Sitena Meriam* (meaning *Our Lady Meriam*). This is not a "Christian festival". The festival lasts the typical Egyptian octave-week (8 days). The last day of the celebration is 16 Mesoree (22 August).

Another title for this festival is **Bride of the Nile**, uniting Isis with Osiris. Isis has submerged—as a symbol of earth—in her husband's body—a symbol of water. This unification is another perfect application of the concept of inner marriage that permeates Ancient Egyptian (and later Sufi) traditions.

=> **It should be noted that from 3 July (the beginning of the rise of the Nile waters) to 22 August is 50 days—another Pentecost.**

9.16 ISIS' (MARY'S) BIRTHDAY

The Ancient Egyptians followed the Sothic year, a period of 365.25636 days. Besides the adjustments made for the 0.00636 days per year, the Ancient Egyptians divided the year into 12 equal months of 30 days each and added five (plus one every 4 years) extra days. These extra days currently begin on 6 September. In typical Egyptian story form, five neteru (gods, goddesses) were born on each of the five days—Osiris, Isis, Seth, Horus Behdety (Apollo), and Hathor.

The Nativity of the Virgin Mary is celebrated in the Orthodox Church on the Eve of 8 September, which is Isis' "birthday", as the second of 5 deities born in the 5 "extra days".

Isis' role in the Egyptian Model Story and the biblical story of the Virgin Mary are strikingly similar; for both were able to conceive without male impregnation. Horus was conceived and born after the death of Isis' husband and, as such, Isis was revered as *the Virgin Mother*.

=> <u>40 days after Isis's (Mary's) birthday is the Egyptian Conception (Planting) Mouled.</u>

Chapter 10 : The Egyptian Spirited Fairs (Mouleds)

10.1 FAMILY REUNION

As noted earlier, the reason for the annual Ancient Egyptian festivals are renewals and rejuvenation of the life of the cosmos. Ancient and Baladi Egyptians do not categorize the activities at these festivals as either sacred or mundane. As such, the gay and secular side of religious ceremonies is an essential part of the Egyptian festivals. The sports, games, theaters, shadow-plays, coffee booths, beer booths, sweet stalls, eating houses; the meeting of friends, the singing, the dancing, and the laughter are as much part of a mouled as the religious processions and visits to the shrines of the Walis (folk saints).

The mouled is a family reunion between the spirits of the past—the Walis—and the spirits of the present—the visitors of all ages. Ancient Egyptian texts and the wall reliefs draw a colorful and graphic picture of the way in which the deceased Wali and his visitors met in and near the shrines, which became houses of the joy of the heart on those occasions.

According to early writers such as Strabo, people from all classes and ages attended these festivals. Herodotus stated that 700,000 people attended the joyful festival (mouled) of Bast (Bastet), right outside Zagazig in the Nile Delta.

In addition to the reunion between the Wali and the people, the mouled allows for other various kinds of reunions, such as:

- Between the local mystic (Sufi) fellowship and other fellowships. Mystics come from various regions, near and far, to participate in the festivities/ceremonies.

- Between various people from local, regional, and national regions who attend the mouled. Attendees include all family members.

- Between old friends who have not seen each other for a while.

- Between old foes who must resolve their animosities and start a renewed friendship in the name of the venerated Wali. People forgive past fights/disagreements and start a new page. The mouled reinforces and strengthens the social fabric—it is a societal renewal.

The main objectives of these mouleds' attendants are:

- Visiting the Wali at his shrine, in order to participate in the rejuvenation of the cosmic cycles.

- To acquire a blessing and a friend and intercessor in the heavenly court by vowing to donate goods or perform a service on behalf of the Wali.

- To recreate and refresh the soul and body with thankful joy, and to take part in the amusements.

- To recruit new members for mystical fellowships.

10.2 THE MOULEDS' OVERALL PLAN OF ACTIVITIES

Early Greek and Roman writers have confirmed the organized and orderly nature of the Ancient Egyptian festivals. Plato adopted the Egyptian model of festivities in *Laws VII* (798e-799b), where he states:

> *ATHENIAN: Well, can any of us find a better device for this purpose than that employed in Egypt?*

> *CLINIAS: And what is that?*

ATHENIAN: . . . First, the festivals must be fixed by compiling an annual calendar to show what feasts are to be celebrated, at what dates, and in honor of what deities, sons of deities, or spirits, respectively.

Next, certain authorities must determine what hymn is to be sung on the feast of each divinity, and by what dances the ceremony of the day is to be graced. When this has been determined, the whole citizen body must do public sacrifice to the Destinies and the entire pantheon at large, and consecrate each hymn to its respective god or other patron by solemn libation. If any man tries to introduce hymn or dance into the worship of any deity in contravention of these canons, the priests of either sex, acting in conjunction with the curators of law, shall have the warrant both of religion and law in excluding him from the festival;

All the elements and rules governing the Ancient Egyptian festivals, as reported by Plato, are exactly applicable to present-day mouleds with organized and detailed schemes.

Such festival traditions were present in Egypt, long ago. Hepzefi's tomb from Asyut, dating from the Middle Kingdom (ca. 2000 BCE), contains ten documents specifying:

- The dates of several types of festivities. Some festivals are to be held annually, others are held seasonally, and some festivals are observed centuries apart.

- The course of the procession between different shrines and temples for each festival day, and the activities required at each shrine/temple.

- Activities/actions on every day of the festivities during its octave duration(s), such as performances of specific rituals and recitations as well as the amounts and types of offerings at each shrine.

- Time of day/night for each ritualistic activity.

- The lighting scheme during the light vigil and the ritual of kindling the light of torches, which are carried in the procession.

- The festive atmosphere of music, dance, entertainment, games, sports, etc.

The present-day mouled is, likewise, a picturesque ceremony with merry sights and tonic atmosphere, even though all such activities are totally forbidden in Islam. The streets are crowded with happy and orderly people. Streets and shops are gaily decorated and brightly lit.

No two mouleds are exactly alike. In general, the primary activities in the Egyptian festivals (mouleds) are:

> a. The opening ceremonies.
> b. Ongoing rituals.
> c. Visitation by the public to the shrine.
> d. Sacrificial Animals.
> e. Public offerings.
> f. Boy circumcisions (initiations).
> g. Lively entertainment.
> h. Lively games and sports.
> i. The climactic Octave Eve activities.
> j. The closing ceremonies—the Final Procession.

10.2.a. The Opening Ceremonies

On the opening day, the present leader of the mystical (Sufi) fellowship that is associated with the celebrated Wali leads a special procession towards the shrine of the Wali. This leader is frequently a spiritual or blood descendant (or both) of the Wali.

The Egyptian term for this procession is *'zaffa'* or *'urs'*, which literally means a *wedding procession* for the purpose of consummating a marriage. The term zaffa has a subtle reference to the unitive action—the inner marriage between the self (Ka), the personage of the Wali, and his soul (Ba). This idea is expressed in Sufi poetry as sexual intercourse and becoming one; hence the term zaffa—a procession to be wed.

The modern concept that the soul (**Ba**) visits the shrine (**Ka**) on specified days conforms to a well-known vignette in *The Book of the Coming Forth by Light/Day* (wrongly known as *The Book of the Dead*), depicting the soul (Ba) in the form of a bird, descending the shaft in order to unite with the Ka of the deceased. This concept is to be found in Egyptian religious texts of all periods.

The objective of the zaffa (procession) is to perform an inaugural ceremony to "awaken" the Wali through the inner marriage of his Ka (represented in a relic of his choice) and his Ba (the soul).

The zaffa consists of members of the local mystical (Sufi) fellowship who don't walk, but rather move in rhythmic dancing strides. They are accompanied by musicians, dancers, lantern bearers, incense bearers, etc.

At the head of the zaffa is one of the most venerable of the fellowship, playing the Egyptian *nay* (a sort of flute). In Ancient Egypt, the procession was also usually headed by a flute-player, according to Herodotus. Other members of the fellowship play other musical instruments. In these festivals, music was required in ritual performances, just like modern times, and was, according to Apuleius, of a spiritual character. It was/is called *samaa*, which was/is an Ancient Egyptian term meaning *to unite through sound/ music*.

The zaffa follows a specific route with specific rituals. It generally takes an average of two hours, but could be much longer. The route typically includes pauses at certain places and shrines in the district for recitations and other rituals at the shrines of the other Walis, to heighten the collective energies in the ceremonies. The procession may occasionally be punctuated by special exhibitions of ritual dancing, including whirling—usually with music – and, at night, with lanterns and many other illuminating devices.

Ancient Egyptian tombs show choirs of male and female singers approaching the shrine. The female singers wave sistra and necklaces; the male singers mark the measure by clapping their hands. The lord of the shrine awaits the choirs, which sing songs ending with special recitations.

The local mystical (Sufi) fellowship leads the procession to the shrine and circles it seven times. Then they enter the shrine, purifying it with incense and reciting certain formulas (spells). In their rituals, these mystical (Sufi) groups connect the past, present, and future through movements, gestures, and facial expressions, in addition to reciting poetry, singing, and dancing. The intent is to facilitate the joining (inner marriage) of the Wali's Ba and Ka.

As part of the present-day rituals, the choir cries, *"**By the power of so-and-so, rise!**"*—reminiscent of Ancient Egyptian's term of prt-r-hrw, meaning *coming forth*, or *a going up at the voice of Horus*. This phrase mediates the call for the deceased, represented as Osiris, to resurrect anew as Horus, representing the rebirth of Osiris. This is the essence of the mouled—to rejuvenate and regenerate the old (Osiris) into the renewed (Horus).

In Ancient Egyptian, **prt** means *ascent, going up to* or *procession to*. The term indicates the intent of meeting souls in higher realms—ascending to them. The name of the ritual given to this ancient rite was **prt-r**, meaning *the coming forth* or *going up*, or *to rise*. The same is used to mean *to rise of the sun*. The call to the Wali is, in essence, *to rise and shine*.

The renewal rites at the temple/shrine are the essence of the ritual ceremonies. The words accompanying the action are of even greater significance. The magic word, the incantation, actuates the power and endows the ritual acts with a magical religious effect.

The magic of the recited word is embodied in two neteru (gods), who represent certain aspects of the powers of Thoth. The two neteru (gods) are:

– **Hu/Hw**, who represents the authoritative utterance, and

– **Sia**, who represents the mind, consciousness, knowledge, understanding, perception, wisdom, etc.

The combined powers of **Hu/Hw** and **Sia** are represented in Ancient Egypt as **Heka** (Hike). As such, Heka represents the ability to transform, by using the right words. The words of power (magical words) are called **Heka-u** (plural of Heka). In other

words, the right words have powerful transformational (magical) effects.

The successful rituals of the opening ceremonies result in *awakening* the Wali. A number of celebrations are described in Ancient Egyptian texts in which the "deceased" plays a prominent role during the festival days. Examples are in two tombs at Meir, from the Middle Kingdom (ca. 2000 BCE), whereby the occupant stands as if he has just emerged from the underworld, happily receiving a festive group of dancers, musicians, singers, and wrestlers, who come to pay homage to him in a procession. Texts next to the depictions read: *for (i.e. to increase) your vitality*. Meanwhile a man is depicted presenting offerings and flowers to the deceased. [More about offerings later in this chapter.]

The presentation of a bouquet of flowers to the Wali at his shrine was/is intended to utilize the sweet scent of the flowers to renew the Wali's life. In Ancient Egyptian texts, there are numerous references to *the sweet scent of the praised ancestors*. In Ancient Egyptian traditions, the neter (god), **Nefer-Tum**, represents the perpetual renewed creation, which is the goal of the Egyptian festivals. As such, the rejuvenated neteru/Walis were equated to **Nefer-Tum**, who is usually seen rising out of a blue lotus.

After the opening ceremonies of getting the Wali to rise and shine, the mouled is officially open.

10.2.b. Ongoing Rituals

The local fellowship that celebrates the annual festival(s) of its founder (Pir/Mir/Wali) is always joined by other mystical (Sufi) fellowships from surrounding areas. The visiting mystical (Sufi) fellowships become more and more visible as the days of the mouled progress.

The various Sufi fellowships arrive in processions with their distinguishable banners, insignia, and colors. Each fellowship is accompanied by their musical choirs and dancers. Whenever a visiting fellowship arrives, multitudes of the laity accompany them, vying with them in zeal and enthusiasm. The mystics visit various neighboring shrines in the area, on their way to the shrine of the celebrated Wali.

The visiting fellowships—just like local fellowships—perform zikr sessions throughout the duration of the octave-week festival to heighten their spiritual experiences with the spiritual presence of the Wali. The zikr takes place throughout the afternoon and evening at the mouleds – mostly by the tree associated with the celebrated shrine – but they can also be held in special tents, public places, and in houses.

In addition to the performance of zikrs and visits to the shrine, all mystical (Sufi) fellowship members participate in all other activities in the mouled—entertainment, sports, boy circumcision, dispensing protective charms, etc. They provide an excellent role model for the young and the old who attend the mouled. They lead by example; and as a result, the crowds are attracted to them and, in most cases, many new members are recruited at the mouleds.

10.2.c. Visitation Obligations

The central religious act at a mouled is the visit to the shrine by the public (men, women, and children of all ages and classes) in honor of the Pir/Mir/Wali. Pilgrimage to a shrine is called *a visitation*, while the shrine itself is called a *place of visitation*. The public's visitation to the shrine during the mouled is an essential component of the intent of the annual festival—rejuvenation. Visitations are conducted every day of the mouled's duration (8 days), usually in the afternoons.

There is a certain etiquette for visitation. The person must be clean and must enter the room by greeting the Wali and asking permission of the Wali to enter or leave. People circle the shrine several times—usually seven, with ejaculations eulogistic of the Wali. They dispense incense and talk to the Wali loudly, quietly, or in silence. Small earthenware lamps and/or candles are lit and placed in the shrines. Flowers are also offered. When leaving, the visitor must ask permission from the Wali to leave, and must say the proper farewells.

People visit the celebrated Wali for basically three reasons:

1. As an obligation and a duty, as explained earlier.

2. To receive Ba-ra-ka of the Wali by visiting the shrine and monument within (*maksoorah*). To receive the Wali's Ba-ra-ka, visitors place their hands first on the *maksoorah* and then on the face. Women use scarves to rub the monument and

then take them home to rub other people in their villages who could not attend the mouled.

3. To obtain special favors from the Pir/Mir/Wali, such as curing illness, getting pregnant, etc. For this purpose, one must make a vow with the Wali [more details follow, later in this chapter].

10.2.d. Sacrificial Animals

One of the most important rituals in the Egyptian annual festivals, since ancient times, is the ritual sacrifice of the bull, which represents the renewal of cosmic forces through the death and resurrection of the bull deity.

We find a similar and later conception in the Abraham religion: Abraham sacrificed a ram to save the life of his son.

The Egyptians connected Apis, both living and dead, with Osiris. He was the son of Osiris, as well as of Ptah, and was the "living image of Osiris". After the death of his body, his soul was thought to go to heaven, where it joined itself to Osiris and formed with him the dualneter Asar-Hepi, or Osiris-Apis. Bull is basically the incarnation of Osiris. Classical writers of antiquities assert that Apis the bull was sacrificed for Osiris since the time of Mena, 5,000 years ago. In the Ancient Egyptian traditions, wine was sacrificed to represent the blood of Osiris.

Egyptians felt obligated to eat the meat of the sacrificial bull and to drink wine during festivities in order to receive divine blessing.

Throughout Egypt (and in all eras), bulls are depicted in tombs and temples, to be sacrificed during the festivals to renew and to rejuvenate life.

The meaning of the English term sacrifice is *to do/make sacred.*

There may be two aspects of sacrifices:

- Unification or what some call communion.

- As a gift

10.2.e. Feast of Offerings

The offerings presented during the mouled constitute a major component of the festival. On behalf of the celebrated Wali, food and drinks are made available to the visitors of the mouled in two ways:

1. Via offerings specified by the Pir/Mir/Wali, and sponsored by his lineage mystical keepers.

The Pir/Wali, who specifies the location(s) of his shrine(s) and the visitation schedule, also specifies the types and amounts of offerings that will be distributed to the needy at his/her annual festivities.

Representations of Egyptian men and women loaded with provisions going in procession to the shrines of their deceased are very common in tomb-chapels, more than 5,000 years ago [as shown herein from the tomb-chapel of Ty]. The same thing still occurs in Egypt. Baladi Egyptians believe that it is our responsibility to maintain a vital relationship with the Walis at their shrines by providing such offerings.

2. Via individuals as a result of special vows.

A person who seeks Ka-ra-ma-at (special favors, but not of a selfish nature; such as becoming a millionaire, etc.) from the Wali must make a vow that if he recovers from a sickness, obtains a son, etc., he will donate certain thing(s) to the public on the Wali's behalf. The moral contract with the Wali (in the form of a vow) is fulfilled by donating to the public and not to any religious authority. If the vower attains his object/request, he fulfills his promise. For example, he might sacrifice an animal and make a feast with its meat for any person who visits the shrine. Having given the animal to the Pir/Mir/Wali, he thus credits the latter with feeding the poor. Ancient and Baladi Egyptians ate/eat the meat of the sacrificed animals, so as to be blessed by the Wali him/herself.

As a result of offerings and the fulfillment of vows, abundant food and refreshments are available to all, provided by the holy host (Wali), courtesy of anonymous givers.

10.2.f. Boy Circumcision (Initiation)

The Egyptian mouleds provide a blessed time to perform boy circumcision, especially during the Tear Drop Mouled.

Boy circumcision symbolizes a new birth for the boy who is being transformed (dies and is reborn as a man), which is consistent with the renewal theme of the mouled.

The initiation process of the boy to manhood can be a private ceremony, with the operation at home, or a public ceremony. Most people choose a public initiation process where the boy candidates are paraded through the streets with their friends in open carriages. The small procession is usually augmented by a brass band.

Circumcision tents/booths are found in the mouleds. The operation is conducted by mystical (Sufi) members of the artisan fellowships and is generally free of charge.

10.2.g. The Mystical Entertainment

As stated earlier, social and entertainment activities can't be separated from the purely religious aspects of the mouled. In addition to entertainment, these activities assist in teaching, rejuvenating, and reinforcing cultural values, as well as preserving societal traditions.

Entertainment options are found everywhere in the spirited fairs. There is always a variety of entertainment programs—animated poetry recitations, storytelling, singing, dancing, stage plays, etc. These programs take place in a variety of theaters, such as a platform outside a cafe, shop, or house; a screen of canvas or a tent; a passage between the buildings; or a huge tent with bleachers surrounding an arena big enough for a circus.

The performers include storytellers, actors, singers, musicians, dancers, clowns, dwarfs, giants, muscle dancers, mimes, etc. All activities are engaging, with the public of all ages and classes participating in singing, clapping, dancing, etc. All the attendants are absorbed and intoxicated by the animated activities.

All these types of entertainment are regularly used in the mouleds to convey knowledge and wisdom. By exaggerating (dramatizing) the behavior of the characters of the story, people can see themselves in these characters, and learn to improve their own behavior. All the different modes of entertainment emphasize virtues and good behavior, the benefits of marriage, family values, work ethics, accountability, etc.

10.2.h. The Mystics' Sports and Games

Games play a major role in the mouled, where people can watch some events and participate in others.

Ancient and classical writers affirmed that games owe their development, if not their very origin, to religious observances. Many accounts of games are mentioned by Homer as essential to the accompaniment of devotional ceremonies.

Long ago, before the Greeks and Romans, games were (and continue to be) performed in honor of certain neteru (gods, goddesses). Such games included (but were not limited to) wrestling and other gymnastic exercises.

Diodorus, in *Book I* (16), affirms such a role:

> *"It was by Thoth, for instance, according to the Egyptians, that . . . he was the first . . . to establish a wrestling school, and to*

*give thought to the rhythmical movement of the human body
and its proper development. . ."*

Here we find again that Thoth's domain extends to the main-
tenance of a healthy body through rhythmic movements and
sports.

The Egyptian mystics (Sufis) are physically and mentally fit. They
display their talents in the mouleds. A sample of games performed by the Egyptian mystics (Sufis) in the mouleds, which one
can watch, include:

- The ritualistic, graceful wooden sword play and dances,
  performed to musical tones of the Egyptian double pipe
  known as the mizmar. The game requires tremendous agility,
  strength, and concentration.

- Display of horsemanship by making horses dance, prance, or
  paw the ground. Also, the Egyptian mystics (Sufis) participate
  in a variety of games while on horseback, such as diverse
  horse races.

- Wrestling games that constitute a perfect combination of
  ritual and sportsmanship. Wrestling is mentioned in the
  holiest of Ancient Egyptian texts, and was considered an
  important element of the most religious activities of the
  Ancient Egyptian festival (mouled).

- Displays of extra-human strength/skills (at no charge), which
  some may call magic, such as performances of mastery over
  pain by eating fire, glass, live snakes, etc.

- Acrobatic and balancing acts, like in a circus.

For light entertainment, the public can participate and enjoy
games testing their strength, coordination, and concentration.
Some unique examples are:

- Crack shots with small rifles at a tiny target.

- Throwing a ball at nine pins (bowling).
- Ringing the bell at the top of a pole with a hefty swing of a mallet onto an anvil.

All other games of luck and fun rides such as the ferris wheel, carousel, etc., which can be found in fairs throughout the world are also found in the Egyptian mouled.

10.2.i. The Climactic Octave Eve Activities

The last night (which is the 8th) of the mouled is a very special evening. Increased activities take place starting around mid-afternoon, including several processions to the shrine of the venerated Wali and other shrines in the district, as well as zikr performances from various visiting mystical (Sufi) fellowships.

Ancient Egyptian tomb-chapels show festive banquets with elaborate preparations that have been brought to the area for the celebration, including carpets, chairs, tables, food, beverages, flowers and ointments.

These festive banquets continue to be held at the end of prominent mouleds, where a great reception is offered/provided for the visiting fellowship members so they can meet each other in a happy atmosphere.

The public becomes very involved in all types of activities on this very special evening, which lasts into the early hours of the morning of the last day of the mouled. The happiness and joy of the crowds is indescribable.

10.2.j. The Closing Ceremonies—The Final Procession

The ultimate "seal" of the festivities follows the Great Eve. It involves the circling of the shrine at noon by the mystic (Sufi) fellowships, who pay their final respects. In some mouleds, the Great Zaffa (Procession) is combined with final shrine rituals, on this last day. These last rites take place during the pulling down of decorations, variety booths, stage theaters, etc.

Most final processions begin in the mid-afternoon at a major square. All visiting mystic (Sufi) fellowships join in the Great Zaffa (Procession), each with their distinguishable banners, robes, staves, etc. They walk in their special way, that borders on dancing, with much zeal and enthusiasm. Some members of the participating fellowships play musical instruments and perform ritualistic dances.

The Great Zaffa also includes one or more ferry boats, borne on shoulders of men or mounted on animals. A small model of a boat is usually hung up in the shrines of many Walis; the boat being called the 'Wali ferry boat'. The boat, with a sort of canopy, is placed on its frame prior to the beginning the procession, and holds an effigy or sacred object related to the venerated Wali.

Likewise, in Ancient Egypt, several divine arks (boats) participated in the processions. The ark stood on a pedestal in the Holy of Holies in the temple or the various shrines, and was drawn in procession by the priests, on festive occasions.

The divine ark (boat), was often called wts nfrw, "the one who raises on high the beauty (of the neter/Wali)". The sacred ark (boat) in Egyptian traditions symbolizes the power of self-renewal. The boat qualifies as a *divine being and savior from the death*.

An example of a typical Egyptian ferry boat is depicted above. Note the presence of the Ba, representing the soul of the Wali, on top of the canopy, which contains an embodiment of the Wali's Ka, such as an effigy or a relic.

The procession of the sacred arks (ferry boats) is frequently depicted in sculptures throughout Egypt, such as in the case of the Apet Feast in Luxor (Thebes). Scenes from an Apet Feast, celebrated during the reign of Tutankhamen, decorate the walls of a colonnade in the Luxor temple and give a lively impression of the occasion.

The present-day Egyptians of Luxor perform the same ancient festivities, starting at the Abu-el-Haggag mosque, located at Luxor Temple, and following the same ancient traditions camouflaged in an Islamic exterior. It is a testament to the resilience of the Baladi mystical Egyptians.

The Great Zaffa (Procession) also includes acrobats, jugglers, wrestlers, singers, dancers, musicians, etc.

At the end of the procession, the climax of the Great Zaffa is the appearance of the Wali's successor (a spiritual or blood descendant) or his representative, riding a horse (symbol of nobility) or a donkey (symbol of humility).

The crowds line up in the streets and fill the balconies along the route of the procession, shouting, waving, singing, clapping, dancing, and laughing in an ecstatic atmosphere.

It is an atmosphere of absolute ecstasy, and the Pir/Mir/ Wali would have not wanted it any other way.

Chapter 11 : Egyptian Themes of Saint Nick's Traditional Festivities

As strange as it may sound, the typical Egyptian festival—ancient and present—is strikingly similar to Christmas festivities.

Let us look at Christmas festivities.

The principal character is Santa Claus, or Saint Nick.

If we ask ourselves what is a saint?

A saint is a holy man

- who lived on earth
- who later went to heaven
- and who comes to earth regularly to help human beings.

The shrines of Egyptian folk-saints dot the land of Egypt from the barren land to the green valley of the Nile.

The Egyptian folk-saint watches over his people, offering his help to those who work hard and do good deeds.

Likewise, Saint Nick. He is always watching to see if you are nice or naughty.

And just as people present offerings to Saint Nick, so Egyptian depictions show people presenting and placing offerings to the folk-saint.[shown below between the trees.]

And just as the Christmas tree is important in the Christmas traditions—where it mediates between the Saint Nick an his followers—we find likewise in the Egyptian traditions. Offerings of food and drinks are left beneath the tree of the saint.

Exactly the same as Saint Nick's traditions.

Likewise in Egypt—where every shrine must be next to a tree.

All types of rituals were conducted next to the Holy Tree.

Likewise, in Egypt. The tree mediates the resurrection, returning back to life.

In the Isis/Osiris allegory, Osiris was enshrined in a living tree. Through the powers of prayers

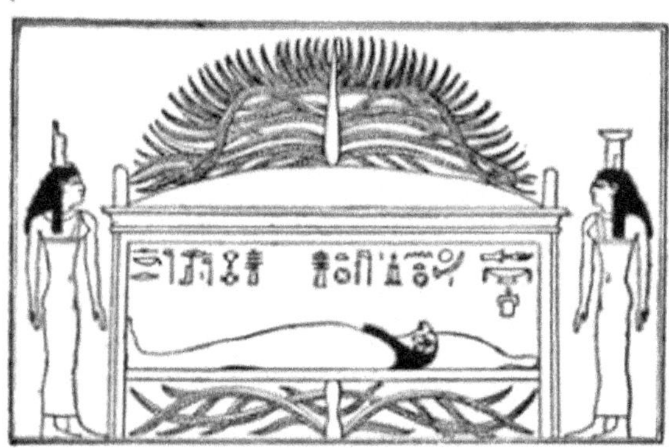

he was resurrected. His green face is indicative of renewal and rejuvenation.

Birth and rebirth—or, to be reborn again—is a constant theme in Egyptian texts. Osiris represents the dying person that returns to life in the form of Horus. This is eloquently depicted here, whereby Horus is rising out of the deceased—Osiris.

The renewal theme is best described in the common saying:

The king is Dead—Long Live the king.
The king is dead—being Osiris.
The king lives on—as the renewed—Horus.

Let us go back to Saint Nick.

Traditionally, Saint Nick rides a sled pulled by reindeer.

References to the gazelle (ghazelle) are widely used in Sufi (and Egyptian) traditions and can be found in countless poems and songs. Since Ancient Egyptian times, the gazelle (ghazelle) has been associated with the region of beloved departed souls.

The gazelle symbolism is found in Ancient Egypt at least since the time of the Pyramid Texts (ca. 4500 years ago), where it shows Horus, together with Isis, Anubis, and Thoth, searching for Osiris.

The Pyramid Texts show that Horus finds his father, Osiris, in the *Land of the Ghazelles*.

In the annual Egyptian King's jubilee (the Heb-Sed Festival) where the King is renewed from Osiris to Horus, we find that the prow of the sacred ark, borne during the procession, ends in inward-facing gazelle's heads to symbolize the region of Osiris —the beloved departed souls.

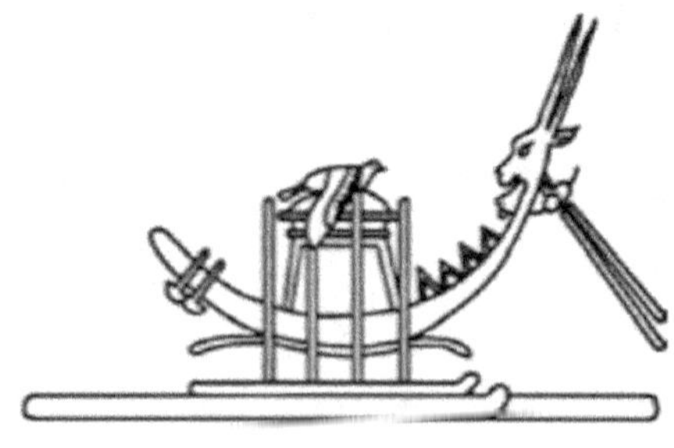

In Christmas traditions, Saint Nick travels in the sky between destinations.

Likewise in the Egyptian texts, the soul of the saint—depicted as a man-headed bird—flies towards the shrine—

to rejuvenate him.

Here this is symbolized perfectly by the flying soul touching the heart of the saint to bring him back to life.

Saint Nick he arrives by descending down a shaft—a chimney—towards the Christmas tree.

Likewise, in Ancient Egypt, the flying soul of the saint descends down the shaft of the tomb to rejuvenate the saint, and brings him to life on specific festival days.

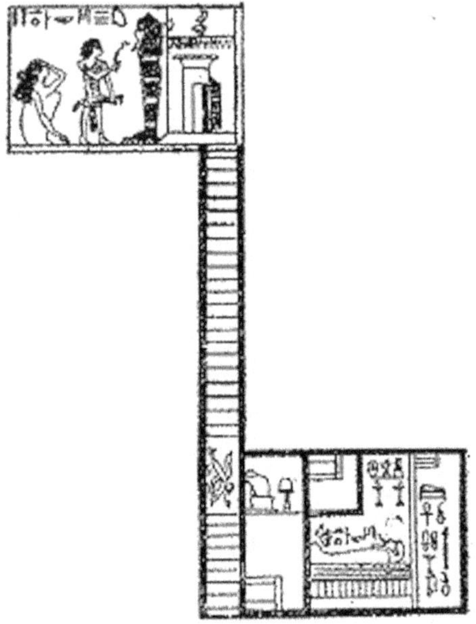

The statue of the Egyptian saint is shown here, coming out of the shaft just like in the Saint Nick traditions…

...and here, the statue of the saint completely emerges out of the shaft.

Refer to the earlier text in this book regarding the typical Egyptian octave theme of festivities and how they are also found in the week between Christmas Day and New Year's Day.

PART IV : COME ONE COME ALL

Chapter 12 : Fellowship Formations

12.1 THE UNIVERSALITY OF EGYPTIAN MYSTICISM

Throughout this book it has been shown that the Egyptian model of mysticism (now known as Sufism) is not attached to (or is an offshoot of) Islam. The natural principles and practices of the Egyptian model are as common in the West as in the East. A mystical seeker is anyone who believes that it is possible to have direct experience of God. The Egyptian model of mysticism is a natural expression of personal religion. The seeker has the right to pursue a life of contemplation, seeking contact with the source of being and reality. The mystical seekers pursue knowledge of the Reality/Truth of God that cannot be gained through dogmatic religions.

Technically speaking, one does not have to be a born/ converted Moslem to adopt and practice this model of mysticism. However, it is true that being a born/converted Moslem is a prerequisite to joining a "Sufi" fellowship in a presently-Islamized country. Such a requirement is caused by fear of the wrath of Islamists in these countries, and nothing more. As a matter of fact, these mystical principles and practices are contrary to Islam, as explained throughout this book.

In addition to the common misconception that "Sufism" is an offshoot of Islam, there is a general tendency to lump very different types of mysticism (known as "Sufism") into one category, erroneously labeled 'Mystics of Islam'.

Egyptian mystical (Sufi) teachings and practices are markedly different than those of Sufis in other countries, as is contrasted throughout this book.

12.2 THE COUNTLESS WAYS

The Egyptian model of mysticism (Sufism) is not a matter of creed and dogma, but rather, of a personal charter. Each one of us is a unique individual. The Ancient Egyptians presented their beliefs in the individuality of each of us in all their texts. For example, there were never two identical transformational (funerary) or medical (so-called "magical") texts for any two individuals. There is no one-size-fits-all dogmatic doctrine.

The Egyptian model recognizes the uniqueness of each individual, and as such, recognizes that the Paths to God are as numerous as the number of seekers. The ways to God are like the streams—they all go to one source. All Egyptian thinking is based on this principle: variations on a theme.

Mystical seekers generate their own kinds of collective life. Likeminded seekers form networks of masters and disciples called 'the Ways'. The framework of a Way is better described as a fellowship. An Egyptian model mystic fellowship (order) can be formed any time and anywhere.

The diversity of humankind is reflected in the diversity of fellowships. Hence, fellowships vary in their nature, teachings, exercises, etc. The diverse nature of organized fellowships follow—in general terms—the nature of the four elements of the universe; namely: fire, air, earth, and water.

12.3 THE PRINCIPLES OF A FELLOWSHIP

All fellowships must contain the following elements:

    a. A link to a spiritual chain.
    b. A systematic organization consisting of members at vari-

ous stages of development/progression.

c. A code of ethics.

d. Modes and programs to attain fellowship goals.

e. An active role in society

12.3.a. A Link to A Spiritual Chain

In order for the aspirants of a fellowship to gain knowledge through spiritual revelation, one or more members of the fellowship must be a spiritual medium who can communicate and connect, through the chain of past spiritual guides, to a Pir/Mir/Wali who is commonly known as the "founder of the fellowship". The Pir is the one who has achieved unification with the Divine [as explained earlier].

Fellowships are therefore organized into spiritual lineages descending from a Pir, forming a mystical or devotional Way. The founder guarantees the availability of his Ba-ra-ka—a state of blessedness implying an inner spiritual power—to the members of the fellowship. Previous heads of the fellowship are known as the Chain of Blessing (silsilat al baraka). The chain of spiritual ancestry unites them with the founder of the fellowship. This chain provides accessibility to the Pir—the power in the sky.

Because of the importance of the spiritual chain, each mystical (Sufi) fellowship is referred to as a *silsila*—a chain. Each fellowship contains an unbroken chain of well-trained guides. The chain began with the Pir—the founder, who selected the most spiritually gifted among his group to be his successor. Later on, this successor chose the most spiritually gifted as his successor (like the Pir did), and so on.

It is always better, but not necessary, for fellowship members to meet in a place close to one of the original founder's shrines, or any of the subsequent heads of the fellowship, as a place of contemplation. In any event, a relic of the Pir should always be available at their meeting place.

Membership in a mystical fellowship is obtained by binding one-self by oath to the head or guide of a fellowship or, if the two do not coincide, to a spiritual master who is himself attached to the spiritual chain of Ba-ra-ka, and who is the spiritual leader/guide of the fellowship at the present time.

The present spiritual leader/guide need not be perfect or all-knowing. What is important is that he is capable of connecting to the previous leader, who in turn connects to his prior guide, etc. The chain is like a pipeline in which each spiritual guide is a section of pipe. The blessings that come to each seeker flow through the pipeline. They flow through the guide, but they are not from him—the blessings are from the Pir/Mir/Wali. The section of pipe for which the present leader is responsible is tightly connected to the pipe- line so that blessings can flow freely without leaking away.

Egyptian mystics (Sufis) don't like to engage in historical or geographical discussions of their groups and founders. If they do, they do so reluctantly, so Islamists will leave them alone. As a result, all fellowships (orders) in Islamized countries have to pay due lip service and "profess" that each founder and their chain of leaders were/are devout Moslems.

12.3.b. A Systematic Organization

Each fellowship consists of like-minded aspirants who share similar natures, mindsets, outlooks, etc. These like-minded groups come from all classes: professionals, tradesmen, artisans, agriculturists, etc. In order to achieve their common objectives, it is necessary for each group to have some kind of organization.

Groups act in the form of circles of disciples working collectively around an acknowledged master of the Way, seeking training through association and companionship. They are linked to the master like soul-mates.

The heart and soul of the fellowship is the person with the most spiritual power/force—Ba-ra-ka. His role consists of a combination of a guide/coach/teacher/soul-mate/friend/pilot/navigator/spiritual medium.

In the West, mystical aspirants/seekers are often attracted to those who write or speak beautifully about great truths. However, in the Egyptian model, it is considered hypocrisy to discuss the truth and not live it. Insincere teaching can weaken or even destroy a student's faith. A real mystical guide practices what he or she preaches.

The members of a fellowship are at various stages of development/progression. Those members, who are more advanced, act as guides/coaches for others. There is not a clear line of distinction between clergy and laity, like there is in Christendom. Each member is learning, and at the same time passes on his knowledge to a newer member.

The members of these fellowships usually take a vow of fidelity and continue to perform their duties as citizens. The members must have productive work to support themselves and their dependents. There is no retirement from the world; i.e., no monks or hermits. The Egyptian model emphasizes a balance between living in the world and seeking spiritual experiences.

Regarding financing in the fellowship in the Egyptian model, there are no required or voluntary fees/contributions. There is no compensation to anyone in the organization. The aspirants/seekers and guides are self-supported by their jobs. Finding a place(s) to meet does not require special financing. It could be a public, private, or semi-private place.

Women are very much involved in all activities in the Egyptian mystical model, are disciples of Pir/Mir/ Wali, and even become Pirs/Mirs/Walis in their own right. Some fellowships in Islamized countries circumvent the prohibition of female membership in their fellowships by establishing a women's section in a voluntary association; but other fellowships make no such organizational adjustments, and women participate outright in all activities.

Participation at all levels in the fellowship is "preferred". However, frequent absences from group activities without good reason would be considered to be a lapsed membership.

These fellowships are not cults. Anyone can come and go whenever he/she wants. Though all members are free to leave a fellowship and join another, or even just leave the fellowship, it is very rare that any do.

12.3.c. A Code of Ethics.

Relationships in the Egyptian model of mystical seeker (Sufi) fellowships/Ways are governed by a noble code of ethics and a standard of etiquette that is essential to traveling the spiritual path. This code is called *adab/o-sool*, meaning discipline, pious courtesy, or the right things to do. These norms, values, and requirements are a critical part of the whole experience which encompass practical daily piety and cultivate gnostic and philosophic vision.

The etiquette encompasses the mystic's relationship with God, his guide, his fellow disciples, his community, and everything in the animated world around him.

Present-day traditions of *adab/o-sool* are an extension of the Ancient Egyptian Ma-at principles that were detailed earlier.

12.3.d. Modes and Programs to Attain Fellowship Goals

The goals of the fellowships are to provide their members with the tools needed to achieve self-development, character-building (virtue), companionship, good counseling, mystical training (spiritual alchemy), and inner experience informed by revelation.

Each guide/teacher provides his own program, as he sees fit, to cultivate ethical and meditative goals. The teacher/guide maintains a balance between individual learning needs and the group's collective learning activities. The guide is often referred to as the sun and the disciples as planets. A balance is maintained between the individual orbit of each seeker (planet) and group (planetary/solar system) activities.

Programs in the fellowships are flexible enough to accommodate the various natures, speeds, interests, etc. of the aspirants. The amount of social and ritual interaction of the members, and the degree of cohesiveness and group solidarity, are essential for group success.

A guide will help the mystical aspirant organize his/her actions into progressive stages along his/her path. Both the guide and the mystical aspirant establish and agree to a projected plan. The guide explains the plan to the mystical aspirant. Both the guide and the aspirant agree on any needed revisions to the plan, and the final conclusion is contributed by both parties. The guide may cancel the agreement if the seeker does not live up to the plan and/ or refuses to perform required tasks.

12.3.e. An Active Role in Society

The Egyptian model of mysticism emphasizes that the adherents must be active participants in the society. Examples of such active roles are:

1. Members must be involved in society by practicing what they learn. Serving others constitutes an integral aspect of self-development. The individual performance in the society is the true test of his/her success.

2. Shrines of the venerated Walis/Pirs must be maintained by the mystical seekers, so as to make them available for visitors' use. Shrines provide ritual and spiritual counsel, medical cures, and mediation among different groups and strata of the population. The shrines were/are also significant centers for local festivals.

3. Members sponsor, organize, and participate in the rites and ceremonies—both religious and secular—of their respective fellowships, at the annual festivals of Walis.

4. Fellowship members are expected to make journeys to nearby communities, in order to participate in their mouleds/festivals.

The various fellowships set up a pattern of mutual hospitality between each other.

5. As a source of blessings, they must provide Ba-ra-ka to those seeking blessings for their worldly affairs. As stated earlier, any acquired supernatural powers/talents of the mystical seekers must be made available to whoever needs them. Ba-ra-ka is a gift (from God) that must be returned in the form of service to mankind and the world.

Chapter 13 : Isis —The Model Philosopher

The most effective way to convey knowledge and wisdom (and for such information to reach the hearts and the minds of all people) is to organize the information into a well-formed story. The Egyptian story of Isis and Osiris explains practically all facets of life. Plutarch, in his *Moralia, Vol .V,* provided a good overview of the Egyptian concept of Isis and Osiris, with its many facets.

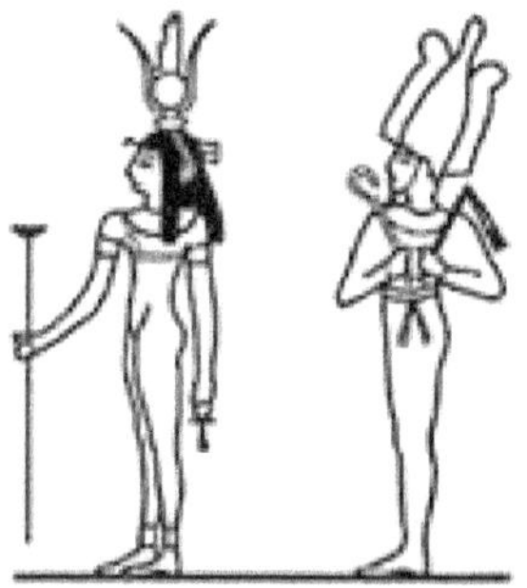

At this time, we will focus on the aspects of the story that relate to the model philosopher (in its original meaning of truth lover) Isis. Osiris is Isis' divine love, described in the Ancient Egyptian texts as the *Manifester of Truth.*

In the Egyptian model story, Osiris, the Manifester of Truth, was tricked by Seth and his accomplices into lying down inside a makeshift coffin. The evil group quickly closed and sealed the chest, throwing it into the Nile.

Osiris died, and his coffin flowed into the Mediterranean Sea.

Meanwhile, Isis, upon receiving the news of Osiris' death and disappearance, was in grief and vowed never to rest until she found the Manifester of Truth, Osiris.

=> This reflects total devotion and commitment to finding and pursuing the spiritual path that will reunite her with the Manifester of Truth.

Isis searched everywhere, accosting everyone she met; including children, for it was said that children had/have the power of divination.

=> 1. To search for the truth, one must go near and far, never leaving a stone unturned.

2. Children represent the power of divination, which is a mode of gaining knowledge that is beyond our limited human senses.

The story goes that one day during her search, Isis requested shelter at the house of a poor woman.

=> This point signifies the paramount feature of the Egyptian model where mystical seekers are taught not to consider themselves superior to others, but to rank themselves as the poorest, lowest, and most humble of mankind.

The story continues that the chest containing the body of Osiris was taken by the waves to the shoreline of a foreign land. A tree sprang up and grew around it, enclosing the body of Osiris in its trunk. The tree grew large, beautiful, and fragrant.

News of this magnificent tree came to the king of this alien land, who ordered that the tree be cut down, and its trunk brought to him. He utilized the trunk as a pillar in his house without knowing the great secret it contained within.

=> This is reference to the Tree of Life, with all that that implies. It is also a reference to the Tet (Djed) pillar of Osiris.

Isis had a revelation in her dreams that Osiris' body was in this alien land, so she immediately traveled there. When she arrived, she dressed as a commoner, befriended the queen's handmaidens, and was able to get a job in the palace as the baby prince's nurse.

=> 1. Isis represents the purified Egyptian mystics, whose knowledge is revealed to them in dreams or in trance states.

=> 2. Isis, the Queen of Egypt, personifies the Egyptian model of mysticism that emphasizes the practice of humility in the world. As stated earlier, in chapter 4, the Egyptian mystical aspirants practice humility by serving others without exception.

Later on, Isis confessed her identity to the queen, and the purpose of her mission. Isis then asked the king that the pillar be given to her. The king granted her request, and she cut deep into the trunk and took out the chest.

Later, Isis returned back to Egypt with the chest containing Osiris' lifeless body. She hid the body in the marshes of the Nile Delta. Isis used her magical powers to transform herself into a bird. Drawing Oeiris' essence from him, she conceived a child—Horus. In other words, Isis was impregnated by the holy ghost of Osiris.

=> 1. This immaculate conception is indicative of the inner marriage that permeated Ancient Egyptian (and Sufi) traditions. In the concept of inner marriage of the self (Ka) and the soul (Ba), Isis represents the bird (Ba), and Osiris represents the self (Ka).

2. It should also be noted that Isis' conception of Horus by no living man is the oldest version of immaculate conception.

The story continues that one night, when the moon was full, the evil Seth and his accomplices found the chest containing the dead body of Osiris and cut him into 14 pieces (14 symbolizes the number of days required to shape a full moon). Osiris represents the lunar principle in the universe and is known as *Osiris the Moon*.

When Isis heard about how Seth and his accomplices cut Osiris into different pieces and scattered them throughout the land, her job was to search near and far to collect and put the broken pieces back together.

=> 1. To bind or tie together is the meaning of the word *religio*, which is the root of the word 'religion'. The action of Isis symbolizes the Unity of Multiplicity—the goal of the mystic.

2. By remembering and recollecting the story of Isis and Osiris, we keep in our hearts a tale that expresses, in Joseph Campbell's words, "*the immanence of divinity in the phenomenal forms of the universe.*"

3. One re-members and re-collects in order to heal and in order never to forget. The most prominent Egyptian mystical practice is called zikr—meaning remembrance.

During her search for the broken pieces, Isis sought the assistance of Anubis, the divine guide, to serve as her guide and guard. She also sought the help of Thoth, who provided knowledge and wisdom in her spiritual path.

=> 1. This signifies the need for spiritual guidance in your journey. Anubis represents (like a dog) the (spiritual) pathfinder.

2. Knowledge and wisdom, as represented by Thoth, are needed in traveling the spiritual path.

Isis, with the help of others, collected all the pieces…all except the phallus, which had been swallowed by a fish in the Nile. She then reunited the dismembered body of Osiris and, with the help of others, wrapped it in linen bandages and mummified it.

Thoth,Isis, and Horus performed the Ceremony of *Opening The Mouth* upon the mummy, and Osiris was brought back to life as the Judge and King of the Dead (the past), while Horus was to take his place as king of the living (the present).

=> This represents the everlasting perpetual cycle of the spiritual power on earth: The King is dead (Osiris); Long live the King (Horus).

1

APPENDIX A: SLEEPING WITH THE ENEMY (SURVIVING ISLAM)

Theosophy was and continues to be a dangerous game to play in Islamized countries. Since the preaching of Union with God is open to the charge of blasphemy (and subsequent death), it was necessary to disguise the mystical principles and practices, to keep Islamists at bay. Islam sees itself as the final and full revelation of God. The mystics (Sufis), under the ironclad Islamic rule, have been suffering and are being killed by Islamists. In order to survive under the ironclad rule of Islam, the Egyptian mystics (Sufis) follow the saying, *"Stay away from Devil and sing the praises to Him"*. Here are a few examples of how these mystics continue to survive Islam:

1. Building mosques next to the shrines of the folk saints (Walis). In other words, they are hiding in the shadow of Islam.

2. Folk saints' shrines in the city of Tanta (in the Nile Delta) and elsewhere contain stones that have depressions claimed to be caused by Mohammed's (who never went to Egypt) foot or palm. Mohammed's foot/palm prints guarantee the protection of these shrines. Even though Islamists don't believe such claims, they are hesitant to destroy the shrines just in case Mohammed really was there.

3. Because music, singing, and dancing are forbidden in Islam, the mystics' (Sufi's) songs, rosaries, and recitations always begin and end with praises to Mohammed and Islam. The large middle part of the rosary/recitation is related to the Wali and the spiritual lineage chain.

4. The mystics (Sufis) were/are able to capitalize on the chaotic natures of the Koranic verses, to find ways to justify their teachings and practices. The mystics (Sufis) became more familiar with the Koran than Islamists; quoting Koranic verses out of context, finding cracks in the Islamic doctrine, and using them very well in defense of their practices.

5. To appease Islamists, the ecstatic practice of zikr begins and ends by paying homage to Mahammed, his family members, and Allah. Zikr is contrary to Islamic doctrine [also see Chapter 1].

6. The mystics (Sufis) use the figurative style in their expressions as a mask for mysteries that they desired to keep secret. They also use oblique meanings for common words, in order to throw off Islamists and as a protection against accusations of heresy or civil disobedience.

7. The mystics dress up mystical (Sufi) concepts in an Islamic garment and generously give the credit to Islam and Mohammed. As a result, they pay an exaggerated deference to the Islamic "Prophet" and to his cousin Ali, in order to keep on good terms with Islamists. As such, they assert (contrary to Islamic doctrine) that Sufism had its rise in Mohammed himself, and that all the mystical (Sufi) fellowships trace their lines of succession back to him and his four successors. The mystics (Sufis) assert (contrary to the Islamic doctrine) that Mohammed has been the recipient of a two-fold revelation: one embodied in the contents of the Koran; the other within his heart. The former was meant for all and is binding on all; the latter was to be transmitted to the chosen few through lines of succession.

8. They state that the human being to whom God granted the most Ba-ra-ka is said to be Mohammed, who passed it on to his descendants, commonly known as *shurfa* (meaning 'nobles').

9. They generally identify the "Complete/Perfect Man" as Adam, but sometimes (to appease Islamists even more) they say it is Mohammed!

10. The origin of all mystical (Sufi) Ways in Egypt are claimed to come from other countries, to appease Egypt's Arab/Moslem invaders. It is therefore claimed that each major **Wali** spent time in Saudi Arabia, Iraq, Morocco, etc., in order to appease the Islamic rulers from these places.

11. Celebrating Mohammed's immediate family members' birthdays, among thousands of purely non-Islamic Ancient Egyptian festivals (mouleds), is a ploy to appease Islamists.

12. All Ancient Egyptian festivals have been continued under "Islamized names".

13. Reading/reciting the Koran (usually at the beginning and very end of the mouled, zikr, etc.) is a camouflage for non-Islamic activities.

14. Ancient Egyptian folkloric stories survived Islamic rule by changing the names of characters and places. For example, a common Egyptian-told story of The Shah of Persia and his Daughter is almost exactly like the tale told to Herodotus about Menkaura (Mykerinos), his daughter, and the golden image of a cow.

15. The mystics (Sufis) use the "Islamic term" sheikh to refer to revered **Wali/ Pir/Mir**.

16. Mystics appease Islamists by telling them that pilgrimages to the Walis during mouleds are a substitute for those who cannot make the annual Islamic pilgrimage to Mecca.

2

APPENDIX B: ZIKR—THE ECSTATIC PRACTICE

Prologue

We are unaware of the existence of most of our surroundings, which we do not see and hear because their frequencies are faster/slower than the sound and light frequencies that our senses can detect. Even though our human faculties are perceptive, they are nevertheless limited, like a radio that can only receive certain electromagnetic waves and not other parts of this band. Our senses are most familiar with matter, the densest form of energy. Lighter and faster forms of existence are beyond our sensory capacities. The perceived world is, therefore, a distortion.

The goal of traveling the Path aims at dispersing the veils that hide the self from the Real and thereby become transformed or absorbed into undifferentiated Unity. The zikr practice provides the means for a purified mystical seeker to close the gap between the physical realm/nature and metaphysical nature. Zikr is a particular method of approach to Reality, making use of intuitive and emotional spiritual faculties which are generally dormant and latent unless called into play through training, under guidance.

Zikr is the central ritual of the Egyptian mystics. This practice leads to the freeing of oneself from the body and the limitation of human senses. As a result, the participant's consciousness is raised, whereby the mystical seeker achieves knowledge of God by way of revelations where states of visionary ecstasy exist.

Early Sufi traditions acknowledge that zikr was introduced into Islamized Sufism by the Egyptian Dhu 'l-Nun al-Misri, who said: "zikr is the absence from oneself (by recollecting God alone)." The absence from oneself is the ideal recollection of God. The whole of Egyptian mysticism rests on the belief that when the individual self is lost, the Universal Self is found. The purified mystics strive for loss of self and absorption into the Divine, in order to obtain personal illumination and transcendence—an ecstatic visionary.

There are three terms for this practice. All three terms describe various aspects of the same practice. The following are the meanings of each term:

Zikr—means testifying or remembrance. Implicit in the term remembrance is the notion that we are coming back to what we once knew (through our past lives)—what we have already learned. Remembrance is achieved by each's heart and tongue [also see Appendix A].

Hadra—means presence; i.e. being in the presence of spirits in higher realms, or calling on higher spirits. The response and participation of these higher spirits in the zikr are very important, as will be detailed later. The goal of the zikr/hadra is to achieve ecstatic trance when the soul is drawn to and is absorbed for a time in the "All-Soul", like a magnet.

Samaa—which, in the Ancient Egyptian language, means to unite through sound/music. As stated earlier, Sufi traditions acknowledge that appropriate music is the means of transmission and intermediation between human and Divine. Samaa is the effective method/way to fulfill the desire to unite/vanish into God. In other words, the right musical compositions and sound of words/names induce a state of ecstasy. The Egyptian Dhu 'l-Nun el-Masri said, of samaa: "Those who listen with their souls can hear the heavenly music/call."

It should be noted that the concept of *samaa* is also very important in mouleds [see Chapter 10 for more details].

What is Zikr?

Zikr is a practice performed by a group of mystical seekers, by chanting, rhythmic gestures, dancing, and deep breathing. While performing their ritualistic dance, the group repeats words and phrases, accompanied by a well-trained choir performing instrumental and vocal music. In zikr, the accompanying singing of well-composed musical rosaries helps achieve the trance. The music sets the rhythm (beat), which is altered by the conductor/ guide to achieve the trance conditions needed to achieve ecstatic visions.

The bodily movements of zikr participants are linked to a thought and a sound, or a series of sounds. The movements develop the body, the thought focuses the mind, and the sound fuses the two and orients them towards a consciousness of divine contact.

The representational sacred dance of the zikr is analogous to the movements of the cosmos and the oneness of the universe. The individuals performing the zikr—as led by their guide – are like the planets of a solar system. In other words: the guide/leader is the sun and the participant seekers are the planets—each in his own orbit—yet, they are held in unison by their guide/ leader.

Like the dancing planets, the mystical seekers (Sufis) participating in the zikr become both ritual subjects/agents and ritual objects. They become so in the repetition of the most economical and condensed of symbols—the word. As explained in items 3 and 4 of Appendix A, it is not only the word of Divinity, but the logos; the word that, in a mysterious sense, is Divinity. [More details follow, later.]

Who Does it?

This mystical exercise is only valuable to the seekers who have:

1. Completed the first stage of purification—both outer and inner, as detailed earlier.
2. Sharpened their powers and abilities by advancing in basic practices, as detailed earlier.
3. Joined and incorporated themselves into a mystical fellowship where they found and bonded with a spiritual guide.
4. Learned, comprehended, and practiced the fundamentals of the spiritual Path.

Men may participate alone; but women may join in. Women sometimes prefer to have their own performance. The musicians and singers in zikr can be either men or women.

Where is it done?

Zikr may be performed privately, publicly, or semi-privately. It can be performed inside or outside a building. The most preferred place is at the 'sacred' tree near the shrine of the Pir/Mir/Wali. A personal relic of the Wali is always present where the zikr is performed.

The place where the zikr is held must be clean and purified by libation and the burning of incense prior to the performance of zikr.

When is it Done?.

Zikr is usually practiced once or twice a week, on specific days of the week; usually on Friday eve. Thursday night is the night that is especially sacred to the Egyptian Baladi and their mystics, for visiting the shrines and practicing religious rites.

Zikr performances by the various mystical (Sufi) fellowships are an essential ritual during the mouleds, as detailed earlier.

How is it done?

Pre-Zikr Preparation

Before performing group zikr, the participant seekers must prepare for it. Such preparation is misunderstood by some writers as "individual/solitary zikr". The preparatory work prior to zikr performance is basically as follows:

1. The mystical seeker must be clean (bathed, shaved, etc.), wearing clean clothes.

2. The mystical seeker must perform the inner purification rituals by the recitation, either aloud or in a whisper, of certain litanies as prescribed by the leader of the zikr. The process includes the spiritual ingestion of established formulas sometimes with the slow swaying of the body or inclination of the head in rhythmic cadence until the requisite number—as determined by the group guide—has been completed.

3. The mystical seeker must then concentrate all his bodily senses, expel all preoccupations and wayward impulses of the heart, and concentrate by any means. A common mode of concentration is to close the eyes, keep the lips tightly sealed, and press the tongue against the roof of one's mouth.

4. The participant seeker must then increase his focus to prepare for an out-of-body experience by entering a dark, isolated place and/or blindfolding one's eyes. Some mystical seekers lie down in a makeshift coffin and imagine that his/her soul hovers over his/her body.

5. While concentrating as mentioned above, the mystical seeker next performs an exercise commonly known as the "guide exercise," where the seeker concentrates intensely on the guide/leader, keeping his image in mind even though he is absent from the room. The seeker who has established a special bond with his guide allows himself to pass away (be absorbed) into the guide. In other words, the mystical seeker forgets his existence (his I-ness) and melts/vanishes into his guide.

The Spiritual Guide and the Heavenly Ladder

Performing zikr causes the participants to enter frontiers that are beyond our normal earthly existence. Therefore, each zikr practice must be controlled completely by an experienced leader and his assistants. As the master of ceremony, the leader guides the zikr and gives instructions by gestures, clapping, a word, a phrase, etc., in order to achieve full vocal and dance coordination between the members of the group performing the zikr and the supporting choir of singers and musicians.

The leader of the zikr is selected for his humility and spirituality. He must be full of concentration and self-examination. He should be moderate and not let the zikr go overly long; nor let it be so short that the heart is not awakened – for the goal of group zikr is the awakening of the heart. If it appears that the zikr has over-excited some or most of the participants, he changes the rhythm. He must watch that the assembly remains orderly, all saying the same thing and using the same voice and movement.

The paramount function of the zikr leader is his role as a spiritual medium to empower each participant seeker with divine tools, to allow each of them to reach higher in order to gain gnosis for themselves. He provides each of the zikr participants the opportunity to climb to higher realms—a heavenly ladder, so to speak—in order for them to gain knowledge beyond the limitations of their human senses. The leader of the zikr, in his person, represents, through the chain of blessing (the silsila of Ba-ra-ka), the continuation of the mystic (Sufi) fellowship through time. He contains the past, and is the promise of the future. He is the conduit to whom grace has passed through the spiritual chain, and from whom it will pass to his successors.

The main goal of spiritual advancement in the Egyptian model is achieved in a communalistic fashion through the spirits of the spiritual guide/leader, the lineage chain, the founder (Wali), and each other. By virtue of his powers, the guide/leader becomes an active magnetic pole/focal point, connecting and activating each mystical seeker into his orbit of influence so as to allow the spirits of the mystical seekers to connect to the chain of Ba-ra-ka.

A fair summary of the process through which a mystic attains visionary ecstacy with the help of the leader of the zikr is:

1. The seeker loses himself into the leader/guide and the leader receives him into himself. The seeker must become mentally absorbed in the guide/leader through a constant meditation and contemplation of him. This is carried to such a degree that he sees the guide in all men and in all things. The guide assists mentally so that the aspirant's spirit becomes bound to his own.

2. Next, the combined spirit of the zikr leader and the mystical aspirant loses its united spirit into the spirit of the last departed guide of the fellowship. This is made possible because the present leader established a spiritual bond with the last deceased guide, while he was alive. It is therefore possible for the present leader to concentrate on his prior guide. A successful rendezvous will allow the melting down (self-annihilation) of the seeker-guide combined spirit into the previous guide—and thus allows each mystical seeker the opportunity to gain gnosis at that level.

The seeker (being absorbed into the present guide) is led, through the spiritual aid of the last deceased guide, up through the chain of the departed successive leaders of the spiritual lineage of each fellowship.

3. If the seeker succeeds in reaching, learning, and comprehending on a certain level, his success will lead him to a higher realm, where he has the opportunity to learn even more.

4. Eventually, the seeker is helped to pass over to the spiritual influence of the long-deceased Pir or original founder of the fellowship, and he sees the latter only by the spiritual aid of the guide. If successful in gnosis attainment at that level, the seeker now becomes so much a part of the Pir as to possess all his spiritual powers. The mystical seeker can then reach the final stage and becomes a Wali himself, as explained earlier.

Progression of the Zikr

No two zikrs are ever alike. Zikr performances represent variations on a theme. Zikr may take two or more hours. In general, all zikr practices consist of the following major elements:

1. The formation configuration/alignments.
2. The pacing rhythms of movements.
3. The chanting and invocations of names, chain names, and words of power.

The following elaborates on the three major items that constitute a zikr practice:

1. Formation Configuration/Alignments

Group zikr formations may be in the shape of a circular or an oblong ring, or in two rows, facing each other. The preferred posture in group zikr is usually standing, although some groups perform their zikr seated.

Men and sometimes women participate in zikr— each is linked with the brother/sister on either side of him by clasping hands with the fingers interlaced and the thumbs raised and pressed together, the hands veiled by their sleeves. The spirits of the participants affect each other and are able to communicate with each other, as well as with their leader. This spiritual communication/connection is possible because the participant mystics have achieved a purified state [see Chapter 4] and because the presiding leader unites the participants' actions and souls.

By holding the hand of the zikr's leader, each participant is able, through the leader's spirit, to enter into zikr in a manner more profound than usual. Nonetheless, even without physical contact, the spirits of the participants in

zikr affect each other through the spiritual powers of the presiding leader of
the zikr.

2. The Pacing Rhythm of Movements

In zikr, there are two primary movement patterns—a revolving horizontal
pattern and a vertical bowing pattern. Zikr begins with a slow and solemn
beat, but typically the pace is quickened.

First, the participants rock back and forth. Then they sway rhythmically
from side to side, nod their heads, or bend backward and forward as they
chant. The presiding leader beats time by clapping his hands. Then the
rhythm quickens, and they rock right and left while their feet stay on the
ground. The guide/leader or his representative controls the rhythm. The
speed of the chanting, and the crescendo to awaken the hearts of the participants, inflames their feelings and stirs their innermost secret parts. The
rhythm quickens for 10-15 minutes; then it slows down.

The zikr is marked by a series of climaxes with soft breathing in between
such climaxes, rather than a gradual building up to one particular moment
which might be described as the central vital instant or section of the entire
practice. These climaxes are both physical, expressed in the increasing vigor
of bodily movements and vocal crescendo; and emotional, intensified by
other elements such as the recitation of hymns (rosaries) and the changing
rhythms of music and action.

As each section of the zikr succeeds another section, all the actions of the
members should be in consort so that there is unity of performance in every
respect. The group framework for the individual (seeker) experience is associated with an emphasis on the harmony and order of the group as a whole.
All movements in the different stages of the zikr should be made in unison
by all the mystical seekers in the group.

The guide and his assistants carefully control the strong possibility of hys-
terical behavior during the climactic moments. Their function is to regulate
rather than to exhort, and to prevent the group expression from becoming
completely chaotic in unpredictable individual behavior. They are agents of
control, not stimulators of excitement. The assistants walk around the participant seekers, correcting those who are out of rhythm and indicating, by
movements of the hand, the right tempo for those who cannot hear the clapping of the guide, or who are unable to follow it. The trance-like state into
which the mystical seekers move is not an unconscious state, and the individual can respond to guidance provided by the leader or his assistants. They
usually do this with a gentle pressure on the arm, forcing the individual to
cease performing the particular section of the zikr long enough for him to
quiet.

Coming back down to earth

Coming back down to Earth after reaching visionary ecstasy is accomplished through a gradual return to the earthly environment through managed breath control and lowering the rhythm. This process is done very carefully, so as not to cause harm to the participants—similar to the care taken when waking a sleeping person.

3. Chanting and Invocations of Names, Chain Names, and Words of Power

In Egypt, group zikr is often performed, with the assistance of singers and musicians, to animate/"give life to" the zikr. While the participants in zikr perform their dancing movements and recite the Names of God, the singers/praisers sing praises, eulogies, or odes (similar in nature to the Song of Solomon), often of the erotospiritual type that brings joy to the heart of the participants.

The musical instruments mostly used are end-blown reed flutes (nay), double reed-pipes, tri-kanun (zithers), short-necked lutes (oud), kamangas (violins), horns, clappers, cymbols, castanets, small drums (baz), and tambourines.

The participant mystical seekers invoke names and words of power while performing their ritual dance. The supporting band provides the music as well as repeating the names of God or reciting a series of rosaries (awrad) that are pre-determined by each individual guide and recited in special times and orders. Rosaries (awrad) vary in different zikrs and between different groups.

The essence of zikr is remembrance; i.e. connecting to the past by calling and repeating the names of God and the ancestors of the spiritual lineage of each particular fellowship. [See the significance of names, in Appendix A.]

Zikr often begins with reciting one of the Divine Names. In Islamized Sufism, it is said that the remembrance of God begins with the repetition of God's Names. This is reminiscent of the Ancient Egyptians' *Litany of Ra—The Creator*, where his 75 names are recited. [Also see Chapter 5.]

The Invocation of the Name is the rite par excellence. One must eventually see God in all things, and all things in God. The proper recitation of the Divine Names empowers the zikr participants with the Divine Attributes. [Also see Appendix A.]

In order to ensure a successful zikr practice, it is important to maintain unity of breath, sound (chanting), and movement. Therefore, the participants pronounce each name slowly and emphatically, with an elongation of the second syllable, throwing the head and upper body back and then forward with each recitation and maintaining the tempo and unity of movement.

The breathing pattern is intimately connected with sound patterns of Name recitation. The intimate relationship between breath and the potency of the Name gives the exercise power. It also suggests that even where words are not articulated, but reside in the inhaling or exhaling, they continue to deliver the words' power. The dominant symbol of the ritual is manifestly the Word. The Word being inherently sacred, it imparts sanctity to the ritual, rather than being sanctified by it. The most important words of invocation in zikr are:

a. Hu/Hw, which is a name of an Ancient Egyptian neter (god) representing the authoritative utterance. The word is usually pronounced during exhaling—blowing.

The proper recitations of the Name Hu/Hw are closely associated with the various breathing patterns during the zikr practice. The recitation of the Name Hu/Hw sometimes dissolves into a mere grunt. As a result of the physical exertion involved, the participants recite ever more quietly, until all one hears is the breathing of the participants—and the music of the singers/praisers.

b. Madad, which is also an Ancient Egyptian term meaning "to be recited", and was usually placed at top of columns containing spells. The word madad is derived from the Egyptian word mdw/mdu, which means speak, talk, recite. Medu Neteru, in the Ancient Egyptian language, means (Spoken) Words of God.

At frequent intervals during the zikr, madad is chanted by the chief hymn-singer. The ritual's primary direction during the madad is the mediating powers of the lineage chain operating in it, with emphasis on the latest deceased person. By invoking the names of previous guides, the present leader seeks the presence of the spiritual lineage of the fellowship (order). Therefore, the singers/praisers call out the names of the chain with intense emotion, to put the participants of the zikr in the hands of the spirits of the spiritual chain.

The evocation of the word "madad" as an invocation for divine aid (or strength) has a profound mystical significance for the Baladi population of Egypt. Madad is found in Egyptian poems and songs, and is used in their daily lives.

The mystical seekers chant or repeat different invocations over and over again, from one section to another, until their strength is almost exhausted. They accompany their ejaculations or chants with a motion of the head, arms, or entire body. During the whole process, they are fully conscious, like a drunk who feels nothing of himself, yet is totally aware of his surroundings.

To use the same analogy of intoxication, the participants become sober again, with the help of the leader and his assistants, at the end of each zikr practice.

Epilogue

The participant mystical seeker reaches a certain level of consciousness every time he performs zikr. The experience provides him a birds-eye view of the world that is beyond the limitations of our human senses. This new enlightenment allows the mystical seeker to utilize his intellect/reason to understand/realize new aspects of the world around him/her. Gaining knowledge is a continuous process of using both faculties of intellect and intuition, to interact and enrich one another.

The unique diversity, vigor, organization, and discipline of the zikr performance, which is found only in Egypt, has always been noted by Westerners. The ceremony is conducted with great earnestness and solemnity.

Zikr performances are rare in some parts of India and Turkey. Zikr is almost nonexistent in other countries. Other Islamized Sufis talk about it, yet there is no evidence of performances. Zikr can only be achieved by the pure mystics [see Chapter 4: The Purification Process]. Some people in other countries pretend that they have received revelations. True revelations empower the mystical seeker with supernatural capabilities. Examples of mundane evidence of such supernatural powers are foretelling future events and reading minds (for specific details, such as what people did/ate, how much money is in their pockets, etc.). Without evidence of gaining such supernatural powers, the revelation claim is fraudulent.

3

APPENDIX C: REACHING THE HEARTS AND MINDS (EFFECTIVE COMMUNICATION)

There is a human tendency to overlook, deny, or ignore one's shortcomings. In order to learn, develop, and achieve, it is easier to see oneself in his/her surroundings. To effectively communicate and influence changes in people, several forms are utilized by the mystical seekers (Sufis), such as:

1. Storytelling
2. Poetry
3. Songs and dancing
4. Proverbs
5. Humor
6. A combination of some or all the above modes.

Egyptians have an endless reservoir of such forms of teaching/ knowledge. These modes become the mirror in which one sees oneself through different actors, actions, and interactions. These modes cover every aspect of life and are easy to accept and adopt in such friendly/happy formats. All the different modes emphasize good behavior, family values, desirability, the benefits of marriage, harmonic relationships, character building, societal duties, work ethics, accountability, etc.

Sufi literature is integrated into the ordinary fabric of life. Sufi literature, as well as the practices used by its exponents, must be regarded as locally valid extrapolations from a center of experience which underlies its outward form.

Sufi literature encompasses and complements the motifs that negotiate the tension between outer and inner fields of action. For the Sufi, transcendental experience is interested in fulfilling the individual's potential in relation to the world. It calls for the coexistence of spiritual and material realities. Sufism incorporates and complements them. Furthermore, both Sufism and psychology emphasize the importance of the motif of descent into the unconscious; but whereas it is considered the end of the psychological journey, it is considered by Sufism as an initial step towards attaining mystical heights of ascent.

It is in the interaction between them that the theme of equilibrium in literature emerges. The theme of equilibrium therefore means the development of inner levels of perception to counterbalance empirical modes of understanding. To further clarify that concept, it is useful to refer to the study of the outer and inner modes of consciousness. All these modes are found in the teachings of the mystical aspirants in their various fellowships, and are also demonstrated in mouleds. In addition to education and entertainment, there is also the benefit of frequent and regular reinforcing/reminding of good virtues, as well as the transference of knowledge, experience, and traditions from one generation to the next.

All forms of mystical teachings have multiple meanings, depending upon how much or on what level the individual can grasp them. The 'inner dimension' of these teaching modes makes them capable of revealing, according to the stage of development of the listener, more and more planes of significance.

The most distinctive characteristic of Egyptian folk literature is its poetic composition, which makes it easy to memorize. All Egyptian forms of knowledge conveyance are characterized by equilibrium, balance, and harmony between different actions/actors. As such, it is the most successful mode of knowledge/wisdom conveyance and retention.

Storytelling

Stories are better than exposition for explaining the behavior of things, because the relationships of parts to each other, and to the whole, are better maintained by the mind. To convey an idea/concept/theme, the best way is to personify the factors and dramatize the interaction between the actors in a well-designed story.

Once the inner meanings of the narratives have been revealed, they become marvels of simultaneous scientific and philosophical completeness and conciseness.

To hold the attention of the listeners, storytelling contains poetic narratives that are almost always accompanied by music. Sometimes the performers act out parts of the story. Other times, the performance includes alternation between recitation, singing, and acting, as well as involving the spectators in the different forms of the performance.

Poetry

Practically all Ancient (and present-day mystic) Egyptian texts are written in a poetic format. One of the chief peculiarities of Egyptian (and Sufi) poetry is that they almost always contain, concealed beneath their literal meaning, an esoteric and spiritual signification. Examples are:

a. The ecstatics are called "spiritual drunkards". The drunkenness of the mystics describes the ecstatic frame of mind in which the spirit is intoxicated with the contemplation of God, just as the body is intoxicated with wine.

b. Deep emotional love, which are allegorical representations of the yearning of the soul of man for union with the Divine, or its love of and quest for the highest type of spiritual beauty and goodness—an objective attained only when the mystical seeker has successfully traveled the Spiritual Path.

The theme of divine love is expressed in the strophic-type poetry known as **muwashshah**. Despite the "common" attribution to Andulicia as the origin of this poetry genre, the fact is that Ancient Egypt is the origin of this strophic-type of religious poetry.

The first country where the **muwashshah** appears is Egypt—and the date for the first evidence of its presence there is much earlier than has been generally assumed. The first and most prominent writing about the **muwashshah** was not by an Andalusian, but by an Egyptian, Ibn Sana' al-Mulk, who lived in Egypt from 1155 to 1211. He wrote about the format for writing muwashshahat in his text of Dar al-Tiraz.

This Egyptian type of strophic poetry—muwashshah-is a group of rhyming phrases molded into a pattern that consists of strophes. The outstanding feature of the genre – the one to which it owes its name of muwashshah – is the regular alternation between two elements: lines with separate rhymes and others with common rhymes. Meter is not an essential feature.

The antecedents of the muwashshah were to be sought in the same strophic poetry known in Ancient Egypt as **musammat**, which is a poem of very simple metrical structure of several lines—usually three or four—with a common rhyme followed by one with a separate rhyme.

Musammat, is derived from **Samaa**, which, in Ancient Egyptian language, means to unite through sound/music, as mentioned earlier in several places of this book.

Songs and Dancing

Folkloric songs and dances are part of the culture, and they serve both as education as well as entertainment of the masses. The rich variety of Egyptian songs, poetry, and rosaries cover all types of subjects: odes (ghazels), social issues, family values, traditions, relationships, work ethics, wisdom, spirituality, etc.

Proverbs

Proverbs are a type of literature that is distinguished/characterized by con-
cise expression, clear meaning(s), an effective comparison (contrast), humor
(as most of them are), and good writing. Each proverb has obvious and deep
meanings. Take, for example, the saying "What goes up must come down".

Humor

The Egyptian mystics are happy people. Their traditions include endless
funny stories: we usually on and about ourselves. For many of us, laughing
at our faults is the first step in being able to recognize and confront them.
Egyptians are known for their humor, as documented in their Ancient
Egyptian literature and as acknowledged by all their neighbors. Herodotus
described the Egyptians as the happiest people of all the nations in the world.

One of the great bonuses in learning through humor is that even as you have
a good time and doubt that you have learned anything, the lessons penetrate
subtly and stay with you, to come alive when the need arises.

Humor is incorporated into stories, proverbs, poems, songs, etc., but it can
also be presented as purely humorous monologues, jokes, comical stories,
etc.

4

SELECTED BIBLIOGRAPHY

Ameen, Ahmed. *The Egyptian Customs, Traditions and Expressions.* Cairo, 1999 [Arabic text].

Arafa Abduh Ali. *The Mouleds of the Protected (Mahrosa) Egypt.* Cairo, 1995 [Arabic text].

Arberry, Arthur J. *Sufism: An Account of Mystics of Islam.* London, 1956.

Baldick, Julian. *Mystical Islam: An Introduction to Sufism.* New York and London, 1989.

Blackman, Aylward M. *Gods, Priests and Men: Studies in the Religion of Pharaonic Egypt.* London and New York, 1998.

Blackman, Winifred S. *The Fellahin of Upper Egypt.* London, 1968.

Bleeker, C.J. *Egyptian Festivals: Enactments of Religious Renewal.* Leiden, 1967.

Bleeker, C.J. *Hathor and Thoth.* Leiden, 1973.

Budge, E.A. Wallis. *Egyptian Religion: Egyptian Ideas of the Future Life.* London, 1975.

Budge, E.A. Wallis. *The Gods of the Egyptians*, 2 volumes. New York, 1969.

Budge, Wallis. *Osiris & The Egyptian Resurrection* (2 volumes). New York, 1973.

Burke, O.M. *Among the Dervishes*. New York, 1975.

Catholic Encyclopedia, Online Edition, 1999. http://www.newadvent.org/cathen/.

Diodorus of Sicily. *Books I, II, & IV*, tr. By C.H. Oldfather. London, 1964

Egyptian Book of the Dead (*The Book of Going Forth by Day*), The Papyrus of Ani. USA, 1991.

El Hefni, Abd el-Menam. *The Sufi Dictionary*. Cairo, 1997 [Arabic text].

El-Beqli, Mohammed Qandeel. *(Egyptian) Dervishes Literature*. Cairo, 1970 [Arabic text].

Erman, Adolf. *Life in Ancient Egypt*. New York, 1971.

Fadiman, James & Robert Frager, editors. *Essential Sufism*. San Francisco, 1997.

Fahim, Shadia S. *Doris Lessing: Sufi Equilibrium and the Form of the Novel*. New York, 1994.

Farouk Ahmed Moustafa. *The Mouleds: A Study in the Popular Customs and Traditions in Egypt*. Alexandria, 1981 [Arabic text].

Gadalla, Moustafa:
– *Ancient Egyptian Culture Revealed*. USA, 2007.
  Egyptian Cosmology: The Animated Universe – 2nd edition. USA, 2001.
– *Egyptian Divinities: The All Who Are THE ONE*. USA, 2001.
– *Egyptian Harmony: The Visual Music*. USA, 2000.

– *Egyptian Mystics: Seekers of the Way*. USA, 2003.
– *The Ancient Egyptian Roots of Christianity*. USA, 2007.
– *Egyptian Rhythm: The Heavenly Melodies*. USA, 2002.
– *Egyptian Romany: The Essence of Hispania*. USA, 2004.
– *Historical Deception: The Untold Story of Ancient Egypt*. USA, 1999.

Garnett, Lucy MJ. *Mysticism and Magic in Turkey*. London, 1912.

Gilsenan, Michael. *Saint and Sufi in Modern Egypt*. Oxford, 1973.

Greek Orthodox Archdiocese of America website. www.goarch.org. 2002.

Herodotus. *The Histories*. Tr. By Aubrey DeSelincourt. London, 1996.

Hoffman, Valerie J. *Sufism, Mystics and Saints in Modern Egypt*. Columbia, SC, USA, 1995.

Ibn-Arabi. *Sufis of Andalusia*. Tr. By RWJ Austin. Berkeley & LA, 1971.

Lane, Edward William. *An Account of the Manners and Customs of the Modern Egyptians*. New York, 1973.

Lifchez, Raymond. *The Dervish Lodge: Architecture, Art, and Sufism in Ottoman Turkey*. Berkeley (and L.A.), 1992.

McPherson, J.W. *The Moulids of Egypt (Egyptian Saints-Days)*. Cairo,1941

Nicholson, Reynold A. *The Mystics of Islam*. New York, 1975.

Pendlebury, David, Editor (Tr. From Arabic by Nabil Safwat, Compiled by Abd al-Razzaq al-Qashani). *A Glossary of Sufi Technical Terms*. London, 1991.

Piankoff, Alexandre. *The Litany of Re*. New York, 1964.

Piankoff, Alexandre. *Mythological Papyri*. New York, 1957.

Piankoff, Alexandre. *The Shrines of Tut-Ankh-Amon Texts*. New York, 1955.

Plato. *The Collected Dialogues of Plato including the Letters*. Edited by E. Hamilton & H. Cairns. New York, 1961.

Plutarch. *Plutarch's Moralia, Volume V*. Tr. by Frank Cole Babbitt. London, 1927.

Saleh, Ahmed Roshdi. *(Egyptian) Folk Literature*. Cairo, 1971 [Arabic text].

Shah, Idries. *The Sufis*. New York, 1964.

Sicilus, Diodorus. *Vol 1*. Tr. by C.H. Oldfather. London.

Subhan, John A. *Sufism: Its Saints and Shrines*. Lucknow [pref. 1938].

Trimingham, J. Spencer. *The Sufi Orders in Islam*. New York, 1998.

Waugh, Earle H. *The Munshidin of Egypt: Their World and Their Song*. Columbia, SC, USA, 1989.

Wilkinson, J. Gardner. *The Ancient Egyptians: Their Life and Customs*. London, 1988.

Numerous references written in Arabic.

Several Internet sources.

5

SOURCES AND NOTES

Listed references in the previous section (Selected Bibliography) are only referred to for the facts, events, and dates; not for their interpretations of such information.

The absence of several references in the Selected Bibliography does not mean that the author is unfamiliar with them. It only means that in spite of their popularity, they were not found to be credible sources.

Please note: 1) sources listed are the primary (not all related) sources; 2) if a reference to a particular Ancient Egyptian text is used in more than one chapter, it will be mentioned in the first instance only.

The author is extremely knowledgeable of the "Arabic" language (his mother tongue) and Islam, being born-Moslem in Egypt and subjected to Islamic studies all his life.

It should be noted that if a reference is made to one of the author Moustafa Gadalla's books, that each of his book contains appendices for its own extensive bibliography as well as detailed Sources and Notes.

Chapter 1: Egyptian Mysticism and Islamized Sufism

Trimingham, Garnett, Shah (re. Dhu 'l-Nun and Tehuti).

Dhu 'l-Nun – Shah, Baldick, Arberry.

Old Religion – Shah, Arafa, Hoffman, Gadalla (being a native Egyptian).

Magical Powers of Egyptians – W. Blackman, Gadalla (being a native Egyptian), Shah.

Chapter 2: The Treasure Within

Gadalla (Egyptian Cosmology, Egyptian Divinities), Fahim.

Organs of Perception – Fahim, Gadalla (Egyptian Cosmology).

The Power of Love – practically all references.

Chapter 3: The Alchemist Way

Atum/Adam – Gadalla (Egyptian Cosmology), Erman.

Mirror Metaphor – Gadalla (Egyptian Cosmology), Fahim, Shah.

Alchemy – Shah, Gadalla (Egyptian Cosmology).

Progressive Stages – Fadiman, Subhan, Trimingham, Hoffman.

Guides – Practically all references, especially Fadiman, Fahim, Subhan, Gadalla (as a native Egyptian).

Anubis – Practically all references, Gadalla (Cosmology, Divinities).

Thrice Thoth – Shah, Nicholson, Gadalla (Egyptian Cosmology, Egyptian Divinities).

Chapter 4: The Purification Process

Pure Gold – A. Blackman, Gadalla (Egyptian Cosmology), Bleeker (Hathor).

The Healthy Body – A. Blackman, Shah, Gadalla (Egyptian Cosmology).

Getting Out of the Box – Gadalla (Egyptian Cosmology), Lifchez, Garnett, practically all references.

Battling the Enemies (Impurities) Within – Gadalla (Egyptian Cosmology).

The Ego – Gadalla (Egyptian Cosmology), Austin, Nicholson, Fadiman.

Self-development – Lifchez, Waugh, Hoffman, Subhan, Arafa.

Chapter 5: Basic Practices

Concentration, Breathing, and Music – Gadalla (Egyptian Rhythm), Hoffman, Fahim, Garnett.

Recitation of Names and Rosaries – Hoffman, Waugh, Ameen, Arafa, Gilsenan, McPherson, Gadalla (Egyptian Cosmology, Historical Deception), Bleeker (Festivals).

Sports – Diodorus, Gadalla (Exiled Egyptians).

Games – McPherson, Wilkinson.

Contemplation – Ameen. Zikr – Arafa, Subhan, Farouk, Gilsenan.

Enduring Love – McPherson.

Chapter 6: The Way to Revelations

Re – Gadalla (Egyptian Cosmology), Piankoff (Litany of Re).

Dualities – Gadalla (Egyptian Cosmology) and practically all references.

Reconciliation of Dualities – Gadalla (Egyptian Cosmology), and practically all references.

Zikr – Burke, Arafa, Waugh, Hoffman, Farouk, McPherson, Lane, Fadiman, Gilsenan (high marks for his book), Nicholson, Subhan, Austin, W. Blackman, Gadalla (being a native Egyptian).

Unification and Deification (Pir) – Gadalla (Egyptian Cosmology), Nicholson, Arafa, Fadiman, Subhan.

Chapter 7: The Heavenly Helpers

Perfect Servants – Nicholson, Subhan, Wilkinson.

Staying Alive – Lifchez, W. Blackman, A. Blackman, Lane, Subhan.

Shrines – Gadalla (Egyptian Cosmology), Arafa, Lifchez, Lane, Erman.

Chapter 8: The Cyclical Renewal Festivals

Renewal Need – Bleeker (Festivals), Arafa.

Mouleds History – Bleeker (Festivals), W. Blackman, Lane.

Festival Regulators – Diodorus, Plutarch.

Setting the Dates – Gadalla, Plutarch, Wilkinson, Diodorus, McPherson, Lane, Herodotus, Catholic Encyclopedia, Greek Orthodox website.

Chapter 9: Samples of Ancient-Present Festivals

Gadalla, Catholic Encyclopedia, Greek Orthodox website, McPherson, Wilkinson, Lane, Plutarch, Ameen, Diodorus.

Annual Jubilee of Egyptian King – Bleeker (Festivals), A. Blackman, Erman.

Latin New Year's Day – A. Blackman.

Chapter 10: The Egyptian Spirited Fairs (Mouleds)

Now – McPherson, Arafa, Waugh, W. Blackman, Lane, Ameen, Gadalla (as a native Egyptian).

Ancient Egypt – Bleeker (Festivals), W. Blackman, Wilkinson, Gadalla (Egyptian Divinities).

Chapter 11: Egyptian Themes of Saint Nick's Traditional Festivities

Common knowledge as well other references listed in chapters 9 and 10.

Chapter 12: Fellowship Formations

Universality of Egyptian Mysticism – Garnett, Fadiman, Fahim, Hoffman (re. women), Gadalla (Egyptian Cosmology).

Fellowship Elements – Lifchez, Garnett, Lane, McPherson, Gilsenan, Hoffman, Subhan, Arafa, Waugh, Lifchez, Egyptian (Arabic) references.

Chapter 13: Isis—The Model Philosopher

Gadalla (Egyptian Cosmology), Plutarch.

Apendix A: Sleeping With the Enemy

Gadalla (being a native Egyptian), Arafa, Bell, Subhan, Shah, Hoffman.

Appendix B: Zikr

Burke, Arafa, Waugh, Hoffman, Farouk, McPherson, Lane, Fadiman, Gilsenan, Nicholson, Subhan, Austin, W. Blackman, Gadalla (being a native Egyptian).

Appendix C: Reaching Hearts and Minds (Effective Communication)

Gadalla (Egyptian Cosmology), Fahim, Saleh, el-Baqli.